Picture This:

Susan Entz · Sheri Lyn Galarza

Picture This:

**Digital and Instant
Photography Activities for
Early Childhood Learning**

CORWIN PRESS, INC.
A Sage Publications Company
Thousand Oaks, California

For information:

Corwin Press, Inc.
A Sage Publications Company
2455 Teller Road
Thousand Oaks, California 91320
E-mail: order@corwinpress.com

Sage Publications Ltd.
6 Bonhill Street
London EC2A 4PU
United Kingdom

Sage Publications India Pvt. Ltd.
M-32 Market
Greater Kailash I
New Delhi 110 048 India

Printed in the United States of America

Library of Congress Cataloging-in-Publication Data

Entz, Susan.
   Picture this: Digital and instant photography activites for early childhood learning /
by Susan Entz and Sheri Lyn Galarza.
     p. cm.
   Includes index.
   ISBN 0-8039-6886-8 (cloth: acid-free paper)
   ISBN 0-8039-6887-6 (pbk.: acid-free paper)
   1. Pictures in education. 2. Early childhood education—Activity programs.
  3. Photography. I. Galarza, Sheri Lyn. II. Title.
   LB1043.67 .E58 2000
    371.33'52—dc21   99-006882

00 01 02 03 04 05 06 7 6 5 4 3 2 1

Editorial Assistant:	Julia Parnell
Production Editor:	Denise Santoyo
Editorial Assistant:	Nevair Kabakian/Victoria Chen
Typesetter/Designer:	Marion Warren
Cover Designer:	Tracy E. Miller

CONTENTS

PREFACE

Babies are not like us. They are not short adults.
Jean-Jacques Rousseau

Children are not miniature adults. They think and learn in ways that were once natural and familiar to grown-ups but that may now seem quite foreign. Effective teachers and caregivers use tools and techniques that build on youngsters' natural curiosity and ways of learning while at the same time reacquainting themselves with the wondrous ways young children look at the world.

Picture This: Digital and Instant Photography Activities for Early Childhood Learning is designed to introduce teachers to one such technique—the use of digital images in the classroom. The digital camera, instant photography, a scanner, a printer, and the computer are new teaching tools that can be used to create curriculum that capitalizes on the way young children learn, provide a simple way to document that learning, and share that information with parents and other professionals.

YOUNG CHILDREN ARE EGOCENTRIC LEARNERS

Toddlers, preschoolers, and early elementary school students are remarkably egocentric. The young child is truly the center of his or her own universe. Curricula must capitalize on the fact that young children are self-centered and self-absorbed.

Photography is a useful tool for teachers of young children. It puts the children right where they want to be, at the center of the action. Photographs of the children or taken by the children literally put them and their work into the learning activity. Encourage children to explore areas of learning that are of vital interest to them and create a visual record of the activities. Inviting children to select the pictures to be taken underscores the importance of their ideas and fosters creativity.

Young children need and want adult attention. The term *group* usually refers to the whole class, and the activities in this book can be introduced to the entire class. When dealing with very young children, however, a smaller group introduction is preferable. Each activity in this book also provides small-group tasks, one-on-one encounters, and follow-up ideas for parents.

YOUNG CHILDREN LEARN THROUGH PLAY

The value of play is one area that truly separates children and adults. Recreation is what adults do when their more important work is finished or when they have nothing better to occupy their time. Play to young children is something quite different; it is a primary focus of life. It is the process by which they explore the world, interact with people and materials, and learn about who they are and what they can do. Play is the work of childhood.

Infants learn how to explore their world through play: by shaking a rattle, looking at a mobile, reaching out to squeeze Grandpa's nose, and via a host of other sensory and motor experiences. Toddlers are motivated to become mobile, in part, to reach toys or play partners. Preschoolers expand their social and emotional horizons to play cooperatively with other children. Kindergartners and first graders incorporate mathematics, literacy, and problem-solving skills into their play themes.

Through play, children work out problems or conflicts. They assume roles and say words that may not be safely expressed in real life. Children direct their own play, selecting activities and themes that are meaningful to them. Dramatic play allows youngsters to revisit real-life experiences, represent their understanding of how the world works, and develop their imaginations through fantasy.

Most important of all, play is fun. Children spend extended time in play because it is self-motivating. They get what they need out of their various play experiences.

Digital and instant photography allows the teacher to capture learning as it occurs. The activities described in this book involve children actively in the process of learning. Although each activity represents serious learning, it is presented playfully, as a "playjob" or something fun for a group to do together.

CHILDREN LEARN TO THINK

A young child's cognitive structures are different from those of an adult. The only way to get information from the outside world into a child's developing brain, where it can be understood and then remembered, is through the five senses and movement. Young children learn by doing. The younger the child, the more direct learning is needed. Being told about a chick is quite different from holding the chick itself, feeling its fluffy down, listening to its little peeping sound, and feeling it peck a finger. Personal involvement with people and materials is crucial for youngsters because they need to explore the world directly with their senses and muscles.

Adults can help children discover how the world works by providing a variety of firsthand experiences, being there to support this learning, supplying resources, and answering questions. Once a child has had a firsthand experience, she or he has a mental picture of it and can draw on that mental picture in the future. Teachers facilitate learning when they provide a scaffold to help children move from simple to complex, from concrete to abstract thoughts. Quality instruction helps children recall what they already know and build upon that knowledge to go to a new level of understanding.

Digital and instant photography helps young children to revisit their firsthand experiences shortly after they occur and to fix them in time. Pictures stimulate the recall of direct experiences and the use of words as memory triggers to recall these concrete events.

Photographs taken during school events have the added benefit of extending school learning into the home. Pictures and photo-based activities can be sent home for the child to share with family members. These extensions offer the opportunity for additional practice, improved comprehension and recall, as well as language development. They also allow parents to know more about their child's school day.

LANGUAGE DEVELOPS IN YOUNG CHILDREN

An explosion of language occurs during the early childhood years of birth through age 8 years. The development of listening skills, receptive language, and expressive language is vital during this critical period.

Children benefit from conversation about meaningful experiences in which they are engaged. They need ample time to talk and to be heard, to listen to language as it is spoken correctly, and to develop vocabulary. An adult's skillful and timely questions encourage discussion and have a positive effect on children's vocabulary and comprehension.

The activities described in this book put children into the center of the action. By their nature, these multisensory activities stimulate language and encourage self-expression. Photographs also bring past experiences into the present for discussion. The hands-on materials featured in *Picture This* encourage language development because they invite children to select them many times during center time.

YOUNG CHILDREN LEARN HOLISTICALLY

Young children learn best when information is presented to them in context, where relationships and connections are made clear. Material that is presented in an integrated way is remembered more easily.

The activities in this book were selected to show a wide range of possibilities available to the classroom teacher. We hope they will be integrated into existing themes or units and serve as a springboard for future investigations.

YOUNG CHILDREN WELCOME NEW TECHNOLOGY

Unlike many adults, young children are not technology phobic. In fact, they often embrace new technology. They can't imagine a world without microwave ovens or remote controls for televisions. Rather than seeing new tools as threatening or overwhelming, young children are challenged to see what they can make these gadgets do. In fact, youngsters may suggest ways to use the digital camera and computer images in ways that teachers have not yet identified.

Whenever possible, children should be involved in the actual process of taking pictures. This should be done under supervision and only by those mature enough to understand the responsibility. The sooner they begin to "frame" pictures in their minds, the better they will become at finding meaningful images to capture on disc or film. Teachers may soon see an increase in the creative uses of these photographs.

Digital photographs taken either of or by the child encourage further exploration of the computer. Once the digital image is entered into the computer, it can be combined with other graphics or described in a written narrative. Children delight in being involved in these sophisticated skills and the hard copy their efforts produce.

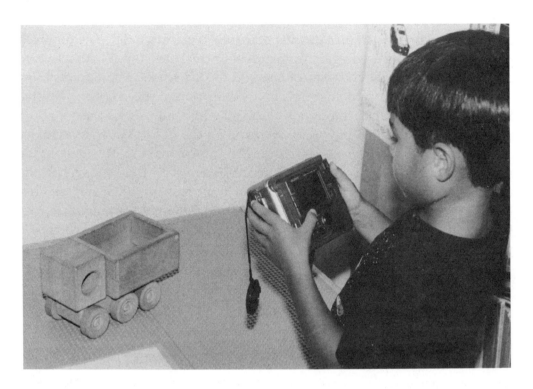

PHOTOGRAPHS PROVIDE FEEDBACK

Effective communication is a cornerstone of any successful venture. Photographs stimulate conversations between all key players in a school. Pictures provide feedback to children, to their parents, for reporting progress, and for staff development.

Digital and instant photography is a natural tool for use with young children because it provides instant feedback. The immediacy of the result provides very positive reinforcement for young children and encouragement to experiment anew.

One way the teacher can use the photographs is to spend a few moments at the end of each day with the children, looking at key pictures taken that day. They can talk about what occurred, the new things learned, the favorite activities revisited, and the human interactions captured on film or disc. Feedback is important for children. These chats give the teacher an opportunity to note progress or to share a word of encouragement to individuals or to the entire group.

Young children are notoriously poor reporters about their daily activities. Photographs of the children engaged in that day's events provide one method of sharing information with parents. A few of the pictures posted in the sign-out area will give parents an idea of what occurred in class that day. The digitized photographs can be used again in the school newsletter to put activities into context and thus highlight areas of strength for the school. Photographs may also be added to a class photograph album, with a simple description of events placed into plastic page protectors and shared with family or visitors.

Representative photographs can be saved for the child's portfolio. A folder can be labeled with the key areas or domains to be examined. Throughout the year, the teacher can print and label pictures that depict the child engaged in one of these areas and that represent either growth or mastery of that subject. Photographs may also capture a child engaging in a preferred learning style. Use the checklists provided at the end of each chapter to document each child's progress and add to the portfolio.

PHOTOGRAPHY ENHANCES STAFF DEVELOPMENT

One benefit of documenting children's progress through photography is improved staff development. As teachers or aides look for proof that a child is working on a new skill or has mastered one, they are furthering their own evaluation skills. They first need to observe the child carefully and then interpret what they see, using their understanding of normal development in the different learning domains. This process sharpens their observation skills, improves their ability to interpret the meaning of what they see, and helps them identify these snippets of behavior as signs of growth and development.

When programs use a formal evaluation system of developmental scales, the teacher needs to understand each skill listed. Proof of this understanding is demonstrated by the activities he or she chooses to record on film. The picture not only shows the child's progress but also documents the teacher's ability to apply the evaluation format to the ongoing rhythms of a busy classroom. This type of documentation is sometimes referred to as *authentic* because it evolves from the child's own learning.

Using photographs to supplement an evaluation system causes staff members to look at each area of the curriculum. Because the teacher needs to report on each domain, there is a greater probability that she will not be ignoring one or more important areas of learning. As the staff member becomes more familiar with the system of evaluation, she will develop a mental checklist that she will carry with her even when not involved in classroom photography.

As the teacher looks through the lens of the camera at a child, she is watching and listening more closely than she may at any other time. She may discover things she had not previously noticed. Is the child exhibiting behaviors that may indicate a "red flag" for developmental delays? Has this child made a developmental leap previously overlooked?

Photographs taken for other purposes can be used for problem solving by the staff. They can share a photograph with the group and probe their understanding of what is going on. They can consider whether what is pictured is developmentally appropriate for children of this age. What does the picture say about the teacher's preparation of this activity or classroom management at this time? They can invite discussion about other ways the situation could have been handled.

Photographs are also quite useful for the self-study phase of program accreditation. Occasionally, the validator will not see an element that is on the evaluation form, but photographs serve as evidence that it does occur.

Finally, the use of photographs can turn periodic staff evaluations into a more reflective, self-evaluative process. Some staff members may even want to create their own professional portfolios. The digitized images taken to demonstrate a child's current level of motor or social development can also be used to show a facet of the teacher's skill. The photographs can document a broad representation of the teacher's work.

USING DIGITAL AND INSTANT PHOTOGRAPHY HAS ADVANTAGES

Digital and instant photography is an effective learning tool for a host of reasons. It is easy to use and encourages creative curriculum development, involves children actively in their own learning, captures them as they are engaged in tasks, and stimulates cooperative social interaction in the group.

Once the computer, printer, and digital camera have been purchased, digital photography is cost-effective. Teachers have the benefits of the pictures without the costs of film purchase and processing. They are also able to avoid the after-school commitment of time needed to drop off the film and pick up the pictures.

One digitized photograph can be used in a variety of ways and in a variety of formats. Multiple copies can be made of projects so that each child is able to take home pictures for extension activities.

Perhaps most important, a photograph of any individual grabs his attention and is motivating. Curriculum that involves and includes a child's own images holds his attention longer than other curricula do. It says to the child and his parents alike that he is a very important member of this class and that we are glad he is here.

ACKNOWLEDGMENTS

Many thanks to the following reviewers for their contributions to making *Picture This: Digital and Instant Photography Activities for Early Childhood Learning* a better book: Mabel F. Higgins, Early Childhood Education Program, Lambton College, Sarnia, Ontario, Canada; Tracey Toms, Assistant Director, Multiage Teacher, The Goddard School, East Norriton, Pennsylvania; Nancy Yost, Assistant Professor, Indiana University of Pennsylvania, Indiana, Pennsylvania; and Kelly S. Fonner, Educational Consultant, Pennsylvania Instructional Support System, Harrisburg, Pennsylvania.

ABOUT THE AUTHORS

Susan Entz is an Instructor in Early Childhood Education with the University of Hawaii Center at West Hawaii; a Trainer for home care providers; a Consultant with a variety of early childhood programs, including Early Head Start; and President of a company that produces manipulative materials for the classroom. A graduate of the University of Michigan, she also holds a master's degree from Teachers College at Columbia University and has completed advanced training at Harvard University. She is the author of more than 40 articles on classroom curriculum and of *Flying Friends*, an integrated science-based early childhood curriculum, and the coauthor of a Hawaiian legends series of six children's books and a teacher's guide that describes an integrated early childhood curriculum stressing character development. She is the recipient of the Hawaii State Teachers Association Friend of Youth Award and the current President-Elect of the Big Island Chapter of the Hawaii Association for the Education of Young Children. Her professional interests include designing curriculum that not only captures children's interests but is also educationally appropriate.

Sheri Lyn Galarza is a Preschool Teacher in Hawaii with Kamehameha Schools Bishop Estate; a Trainer for early childhood students in Hawaii Community College; and a Child Development Certification (CDA) Adviser. She is a graduate of the University of Hawaii and holds a professional diploma in educational psychology and a master's degree in education from Heritage College. She is the coauthor of a Hawaiian legends series of six children's books and a teacher's guide that describes an integrated early childhood curriculum stressing character development. A former member of the Hawaii State Advisory Board for Child Care Services and current President of the Hawaii Association for the Education of Young Children (HAEYC)—Big Island Chapter, an affiliate of the NAEYC, she received the 1999 Circle of Honor Award sponsored by Good Beginnings Alliance Council for being one of the top early childhood professionals of the year in Hawaii. Her interests include presenting workshops and conducting in-service training for early childhood professionals, designing culturally relevant curriculum based on child interest, and developing strategies to involve parents in the education of their children.

To assistant teacher Pam Punihaole and the families and children of the Kamehameha Kona Preschool—Na Pua Class: Harmony Aiona, Savannah Ako, Alicia Carvalho, Josiah Duhaylongsod-Estabilio, Malamalama Ellis, Taylor Fukumitsu, Jenna Henriques, Mana'o Ikeda, Kehaulani Jelsma, Clifford Kow, Shelby Lewis, Kanoa Llanes, Kandy Mento, Kyle Mento, Tyler Parish, Riley Pavao, Chelsea Poe, Kona Verdadero, Hokuloa Waahila, Kalei Watai.

A special thank-you to Barbara Souza, regional manager for Kamehameha Schools Preschool Division—West Hawaii, for her constant encouragement and enthusiasm.

1

LANGUAGE

LANGUAGE INTRODUCTION

What Is Language?

Language is a system of symbols agreed on by a group of people to represent objects, concepts, and experiences. Language is represented by words, and a precise set of rules governs their combination. Language is composed of two parts: *receptive language* (listening) and *expressive language* (speaking).

Why Is Language Learning Important?

Learning to use language is the preeminent human accomplishment. It is important for three reasons:

1. The purpose of language is communication and social interaction with other people. It allows us to express our needs, wants, and concerns; to direct others; to direct our own behavior; to describe or explain events; to question; and to relate to others.

2. Very early in human development, young children learn to think in words. This fusion of thought and language emerges as inner speech that lasts a lifetime.

3. Language is important diagnostically because children's verbalizations provide insight into what the children know and understand about the world. The development of language makes it possible to trace a child's movement from the concrete to the abstract and from a description of the here and now to the contemplation of past and future occurrences or of fantasy.

Individuals with weak language skills face social, emotional, academic, and intellectual challenges throughout life. Poor listening and verbal skills take a toll on children's social relationships. Children with these poor skills often have difficulty joining others at play, maintaining their end of a conversation, staying on track, asking relevant questions, negotiating, or solving problems. Because the consequences of a language delay or disorder are so significant, it is important that help for children be sought when signs are noticed.

How Is Language Learned?

Language acquisition is an intricate dance between genetic predisposition and social engagement. Children are born with the capacity to learn language. But although humans are "hard wired" to listen and to speak, children must have the opportunity to use their equipment. They need to be actively engaged in language-based interactions with caring adults. By using gestures, facial expressions, sounds, intonations, words, and sentences, young children construct their own understanding of language.

Language is intrinsically motivating. Babies gurgle and coo because they enjoy the physical sensation of speech. They quickly learn that these sounds bring a positive reaction from that soft, sweet-smelling person who provides food and cares for them. Speaking is a skill that requires a great deal of practice. Fortunately, it is so rewarding that most children are motivated to expend the energy to do so.

Language follows a predictable sequence. The timetable may vary slightly from child to child, but the sequence remains constant. Cooing precedes babbling and single-word utterances, which predate two-word phrases, simple sentences, and complex sentences. Each affects the development of the stage that follows.

How Is Language Development Facilitated?

A caring adult, whether teacher, caregiver, or parent, needs to provide a safe, secure, loving environment in which talking and listening can occur. Children who are fearful or preoccupied are not available for language learning.

Provide a language-rich environment with a variety of interesting things for children to see, touch, smell, hear, taste, do, and talk about. Language is learned best when people talk about real objects or events that are truly of interest to them. Provide as many firsthand experiences as possible and explore these topics in enough depth to help children develop a meaningful vocabulary to describe their experiences.

Schedule time for meaningful conversation and contemplation. Facilitate discussion between both adults and children and among the children themselves. Encourage children to make choices and decisions, with frequent opportunities to discuss with, explain to, or teach another.

In conversation, model appropriate language usage. Use vocabulary slightly beyond the child's current level, adjust sentence structure to the child's current capacity to comprehend, ask open-ended questions, share feelings, use rich language to direct or describe, and offer opinions. Answering a child's questions acknowledges both the initiative and the effort required to ask it. Formulate answers on the level of the child's understanding.

Remember that young children learn best when they explore ideas in a holistic way. A thematic unit or the project approach allows children to integrate listening, speaking, reading, writing, mathematics, science, and the other curriculum areas in a natural, meaningful way.

Most of all, make language learning enjoyable.

LIGHTS, CAMERA, ACTION

SKILL: LANGUAGE—ACTION WORDS (VERBS)

OBJECTIVES:

1. To experience the meaning of verbs physically
2. To follow directions using action words
3. To identify named verbs in pictures
4. To describe actions in pictures

DESCRIPTION:

Invite children to participate in a particular movement. For example, say, "Let's all jump up and down together. Jump, jump, jump." Take candid photographs of individual children as they perform this motion.

Print, mount on cards, and laminate the photos. Then share them with the group. Have each child select a card at random and describe what is pictured on that card. For example, "In this picture, Jennifer is jumping."

Use the pictures to lead morning exercises or to get the wigglies out at circle time. Have the leader choose a card, identify the motion, and lead the group in that action.

Repeat this process with other actions: clapping, climbing, rolling, pouring, stirring, hopping, twisting, bending, winking.

EXTENSIONS:

Small-Group Activities:

Select six photographs of actions and insert them into a page layout program so that there are three photos across in two rows. Print two copies. Mount one copy on construction paper to make a game board; laminate it. Cut the other copy into its six individual pictures; mount the pictures on construction paper to make picture playing cards and then laminate them. Repeat with several other sets of photographs to make four to six sets of game boards and picture cards. To play a lotto game, place the cards face down on the table. Give each player a game board. Have one child select a picture card and name the action word depicted by the photograph. Tell each child with that word on his or her game board to cover it with a button or paper token. The player whose game board is filled first is the "first winner." Continue to play until all children are "winners."

Independent Explorations:

Place the photographs into a basket for the children to sort. For example, a child can sort them by actions—all pictures of children running in one pile, all those of children clapping in another, and so on.

One-on-One Instruction:

Receptive Language: Place several action pictures in front of the child and name one. Ask the child to find it. For example, say, "Find the picture of pouring."

Expressive Language: Show the child a picture and ask the child to answer a question. For example, ask, "What is _____ [Patty] doing?"

Family Involvement:

Print a set of photographs for each child and send them home in an envelope. Include instructions to an adult to encourage the child to describe what is pictured.

WHERE'S THE BEAR?

SKILL: LANGUAGE—POSITION WORDS

OBJECTIVES:

1. To place a teddy bear in a named position
2. To name the position the teddy bear is in
3. To point to the picture that depicts the bear in a named position
4. To name the position of the bear in a photograph
5. To match pictures of bears by the positions they are in

DESCRIPTION:

Use a young child's attachment to teddy bears to explore position words. Ask each child to bring a favorite teddy bear, other stuffed animal, or doll from home; introduce it to the group. For example, say, "This is Fuzzy Brown Bear. He was very excited to come to school today."

Tell the children that the bears want to show how to play a new game. With your own bear, lead the children through a variety of movements that include prepositions. For example, say, "Put the bear *over* your head, *between* your legs, *behind* your back, *under* your arm, then *on* your shoulder."

During center time, set up a photo studio where individual children can pose their bears. Take photographs of several children placing their bears in particular locations (e.g., "Put your bear *next to* the fish tank." "Hide your bear *under* the chair." "Take your bear *through* the playhouse door." "Put your bear *on* the tricycle."). Print, mount on cards, and laminate the pictures.

Each day during this project, ask a few children to show the pictures of their bears and to describe where their bears are.

EXTENSIONS:

Small-Group Activities:

Encourage children to take their bears to the housekeeping and other dramatic play areas to stimulate their use of position words and include them during play.

Independent Explorations:

Place sets of cards out for children to sort by (a) bear ownership, (b) pictured locations, or (c) types of bears.

One-on-One Instruction:

Receptive Language: Place all of one child's bear photographs on the table and name one of the positions. Say, "Show me the picture of you putting Fuzzy Brown Bear *on* the tricycle." Ask the child to point to that picture.

Expressive Language: Encourage the child to talk to the bear as a parent would to a small child, describing its pictures to the bear (e.g., "Look, Fuzzy, here is a picture of you *on* the tricycle.").

Family Involvement:

Send the child's bear and photographs home and invite parents to look at the pictures with their child and to talk about the positions of the bear. Suggest that they direct their child to place the bear in the home environment by using the same positions. For example, they can say, "Put Fuzzy Brown Bear *on* the sofa."

PHOTO SHOOT

SKILL: LANGUAGE—LABELING OBJECTS

OBJECTIVES:

1. To match three-dimensional objects
2. To name three-dimensional objects
3. To match photographs with their three-dimensional objects
4. To match photographs of objects
5. To name objects in photographs

DESCRIPTION:

Help toddlers and young preschoolers see the relationship between real objects and two-dimensional representations by inviting the children to help with a photo shoot. Put out an array of objects that represent the target words to be learned. Have each child pick an object he would like photographed. Allow the child to help photograph it.

Take the children to the computer so that they can assist in the printing. Talk about the items during the printing process (e.g., "Let's do Kalei's picture next. Kalei, what was your object? Oh, that's right. Kalei took a picture of a snake."). Print two copies of each picture and mount them as cards.

Put out the objects that were photographed and have each child in turn select a face-down card. Ask the child to identify the pictured object and to put it by its three-dimensional object.

EXTENSIONS:

Small-Group Activities:

Work with the group to create a second set of object photographs.

Independent Explorations:

Place a set of objects and pictures in the activity center for matching.

One-on-One Instruction:

Receptive Language: Put out the set of objects used in the photo shoot. Ask the child to point to each object as you name it. Next, hand the child a picture card to be placed by its object. Finally, work only with the set of pictures; have the child hand you a picture you name.

Expressive Language: Show the child the key objects, pick up or point to one, and ask the child to talk about it. If she is unable to name the object, give a clue. Point to the picture of the apple, saying, "It's an /ap/." If the child is still unable to retrieve the word, provide it, use it in a sentence, and then name it again (e.g., "Apple. This is an apple. Apple."). Encourage the child to repeat the word.

Family Involvement:

Invite parents to send to school common objects they would like their child to know how to name. Work with the child to make the set of photographs and send home the object picture sets, with directions for the parents on how to use them effectively.

PICTURE THIS

═══════════════════════════════════════

SKILL: LANGUAGE—VERBAL EXPRESSION

OBJECTIVES:

1. To develop verbal expressive skills
2. To develop aesthetic appreciation
3. To develop self-confidence

DESCRIPTION:

Work with pairs of children to identify objects, people, events, or places they find interesting and would like to photograph. Talk with them about how to set up each picture, whether it should be a close-up or a wide-angle shot. Allow the children to take the shots, with assistance if necessary.

Take the children to the computer, download the photographs into a page layout program, and work with the children to place each picture and then create effects and text for the rest of the page.

During group time, ask each child to share his or her page and to describe it, tell why it is of interest, and explain the process used to create it.

EXTENSIONS:

Small-Group Activities:

Have the children in the group interview the designer of each page, formulating questions and listening carefully to the answers.

Independent Explorations:

Put the pictures displayed during group time in the learning center for individual investigation and discussion.

One-on-One Instruction:

Receptive Language: Play a game of I Spy With My Own Little Eye with the child's own work. Select a photograph to be described in rich detail so that the child is able to identify it from the clues.

Expressive Language: Have each child evaluate his or her work, deciding which is liked best and why. Ask each child to select the best samples to be included in his or her year-long portfolio collection.

Family Involvement:

Assemble the photographs designed by each child into individual collections to be sent home as a source of discussion and pride.

LEARNING LOTTO

SKILL: LANGUAGE—VOCABULARY DEVELOPMENT

OBJECTIVES:

1. To name pictured items relating to a current theme or unit
2. To describe the physical attributes of the pictured item
3. To describe the function of a pictured item

DESCRIPTION:

When considering a new theme or unit of study, brainstorm and list all new vocabulary the children will need. Identify those objects or processes that can be photographed and take those pictures as the unit progresses.

In a separate page layout program, size the photographs to about 1½-inch squares. Insert them into a lotto board format of two rows down and three columns across. Print two copies. Laminate both copies and then cut one set into individual playing cards.

Share the game with the whole group, having the children identify the objects or actions and then showing them how to play the game.

EXTENSIONS:

Small-Group Activities:

Work with a small group to identify objects to use for other theme-related lotto games. Encourage children to name the objects and actions as they discuss plans for creating the game.

Independent Explorations:

Place the game materials into an envelope in a learning center for individual exploration.

One-on-One Instruction:

Receptive Language: Play the game with one child. Place all the individual cards face up on the table. Say, "Find the _____ and put it on the game board." If the child has difficulty, point to two cards and ask, "Is the _____ this one or that one?"

Expressive Language: Play the game with one child. Before each player can place a game piece on the playing board, he must be able to name it.

Family Involvement:

Send home copies of the game with directions written on the outside of the manila envelope containing all the game pieces.

YESTERDAY, TODAY, AND TOMORROW

SKILL: LANGUAGE—VERB TENSE

OBJECTIVES:

1. To develop an appreciation for the passage of time
2. To sequence events
3. To use regular and irregular past tense verbs correctly
4. To use present and future tenses correctly

DESCRIPTION:

Time is an illusive concept for young children, and the language used to describe when events occur is also challenging. Help children develop an understanding of the sequence of events and the words used to describe them.

Make a large pocket chart with three columns. Write "yesterday," "today," and "tomorrow" atop the columns as labels. Glue two or three thin poster board strips below each label. Take photographs of classroom events, print them, and make sentence strip cards to describe the action and the proper tense. For example, write "Yesterday: We finger <u>painted.</u>" "Today: We easel <u>paint.</u>" "Tomorrow: We <u>will</u> sponge <u>paint.</u>"

During group time, show the photographs from the previous day's events and talk about them, modeling the correct verb usage. Place them in the chart. Next, put up the sentence strips describing the activities.

Then show the photo of today's activity, put it into the chart, and add the sentence strip. Describe today's activities using the present tense. Repeat with tomorrow's activities, using the future tense.

EXTENSIONS:

Small-Group Activities:

Form an activity-planning group. Meet with the group to decide on a few future activities. For example, the group might decide on the snack to serve or the instruments to use to accompany a song. Depending on the maturity of the children in the group, they may even take the photographs.

Independent Explorations:

The child may take the photographs out of the chart, mix them up, and then put them back into the correct spot. Make this a self-correcting game by reducing the key photograph, printing it, and gluing it onto the back of the descriptive sentence strip.

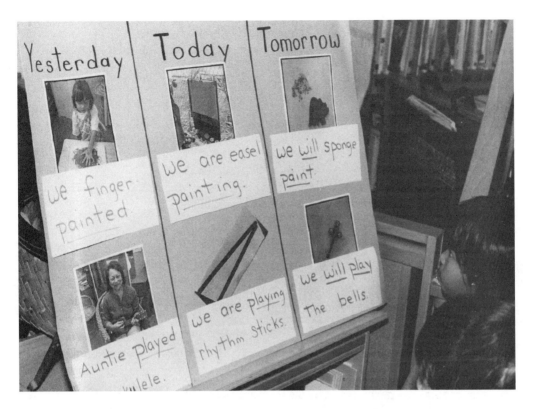

One-on-One Instruction:

Receptive Language: Spend a few moments with the child looking at the chart. Describe one of the pictures, modeling the correct language. Ask the child to point to the named photograph. For example, say, "Yesterday, Auntie played the ukulele."

Expressive Language: Point to a picture on the chart and ask a question that places it in time. Have the child answer, using the correct tense. For example, ask, "What special snack will Josh's mom bring tomorrow?"

Family Involvement:

Locate the chart near the check-in table and comment on it as the children arrive and depart. Encourage parents to talk about events that have occurred at school that day and that will happen at school tomorrow.

COLOR A RAINBOW

SKILL: LANGUAGE—COLOR WORDS

OBJECTIVES:

1. To identify objects of a particular color
2. To name objects of a particular color
3. To name photographs of a particular color
4. To group photographs by color

DESCRIPTION:

Take the class on a color treasure hunt, having children locate in their environment objects of a particular color. One day, the group might look for red objects, and another day focus on things that are purple.

Each day, print the photographs on a color printer. Have the group cut out the pictures.

Make a large outline of a rainbow on butcher paper. Write one color word on the left edge of each color of arc. Then have the children glue photographs of that color into the correct arc. For example, the yellow arc might be represented with a yellow crayon, marking pen, Lego block, yield sign, and cup from the dramatic play area.

Hang the color rainbow in the room and talk with the children about what they have found that represents the targeted color. Repeat each day, focusing on a different color, then locate objects, take the photographs, and add them to the display.

EXTENSIONS:

Small-Group Activities:

Take a walk with a small group and the camera to find additional objects of a particular color. Add these to the large rainbow chart or have the children make their own color card games from the pictures. To make a Go Fish for Colors game, print four copies of each color photograph. Mount each picture on card stock and play.

Independent Explorations:

Prepare a piece of white poster board that has a color word printed on the top and a sample color drawn near it. Provide discarded magazines and catalogs. The child's job is to look through the printed material to find pictures of the designated color and then cut or tear them out and glue them onto the poster.

One-on-One Instruction:

Receptive Language: Look at the rainbow display with the child and name pictured objects of different colors. Have the child find the named picture. For example, say, "Where is the yellow chair?"

Expressive Language: Point to a photograph on the rainbow chart and ask the child to name its color. For example, ask, "What color is this chair?"

Family Involvement:

Send home a partially completed color poster, as described in the "Receptive Language" section above. Ask the parents to work with their child to look through printed material at home to find additional pictures to complete the poster. Encourage the parents to include color words in their daily conversations with their child during this period.

WHOSE SHOES?

SKILL: LANGUAGE—POSSESSIVE WORDS

OBJECTIVES:

1. To identify the ownership of objects
2. To use possessive words correctly

DESCRIPTION:

Use the camera to take full-body pictures of children and teachers in the class. Visitors dressed in their work uniforms also make good subjects for this activity.

Print each photograph taken. Then size the picture so that only the shoes are visible and print this shot. Mount both sizes of picture. Repeat the process to make 6 to 12 sets of pictures.

Show one large picture to the group and talk about who is pictured. Ask the children to name the individual. Then point to the feet of the pictured person and ask whose shoes are pictured. Have the children answer in the possessive form. Then show the group the small shoe card that matches this picture. Say, "Yes, these are _____'s shoes."

Repeat with the other picture sets.

EXTENSIONS:

Small-Group Activities:

Tell the children to take off their shoes and to put them into a container. Ask the first volunteer to choose a shoe and to try to guess whose shoe it is. With the group, chant, "Whose shoe is it?" Help the child respond, "I think this is _____'s shoe." When the owner is located, that child is the next to choose a shoe from the container.

Independent Explorations:

Put the large pictures of individuals on a pocket chart and the individual footwear cards in a container nearby. The child is to select individual cards and match the shoes to the owner, saying the sentence before putting the card into the pocket.

One-on-One Instruction:

Receptive Language: Lay out the full-body pictures of the people. Describe one of the pairs of shoes, asking the child to identify whose footwear it is. For example, say, "I see a pair of black gym shoes with long white laces. Whose shoes are those?"

Expressive Language: Lay out the full-body pictures in this set. Hand the child one of the small shoe pictures and ask, "Whose shoes are these?" Have the child answer in words and then match the pictures.

Family Involvement:

Encourage the family to have the young child help with household chores that require identification of ownership. For example, the child might help a parent sort laundry, identifying different pieces of clothing by using possessives correctly.

I'M THINKING OF . . .

SKILL: LANGUAGE—DESCRIPTIVE WORDS

OBJECTIVES:

1. To listen to verbal descriptions
2. To identify people or objects by verbal descriptions

DESCRIPTION:

Take random photographs of children engaged in classroom activities, classroom visitors, and people encountered on school trips. Place four photographs into a letter-sized page layout program and print them. Cut out these pictures and mount them.

Place the pictures into a pocket chart or display them along a chalkboard ledge. Describe each picture in a series of sentences. Stop after each sentence to see whether the children are able to guess who is being described. For example, say,

"I am thinking of someone who is a girl."

"I am thinking of someone with black hair."

"I am thinking of someone who is kneeling on the floor."

"I am thinking of someone who is building with blocks."

Repeat the activity several times in the group with different pictures so the children understand that each descriptive sentence offers more clues to the individual's identity. Vary the activity from time to time, using common objects.

EXTENSIONS:

Small-Group Activities:

Assign one child to assume the role of leader, displaying the pictures, selecting an object, and describing it. Tell the others to try to guess which object the leader is describing. The child who guesses the object or person first is then the next leader.

Independent Explorations:

Tape-record descriptions to accompany each set of pictures. Put the pictures and the cassette into a labeled envelope near the tape player. The child may use the tape and earphones to listen to the descriptions and locate the described photographs.

One-on-One Instruction:

Receptive Language: Play the game individually, structuring the clues to the child's level of language development.

Expressive Language: Play the game with the child acting as leader and giving the clues.

Family Involvement:

Send home directions for playing the I'm Thinking Of . . . game with the child. Stress to parents the importance of making the descriptions clear and of giving their child time to think of the answer. It helps when first beginning to play this game to limit the range of possibilities. For example, parents might play this game while waiting in line at the grocery story: "I'm thinking of something that is in our cart. It is . . ."

ON YOUR MARK, GET SET, NAME IT

SKILL: LANGUAGE—VOCABULARY DEVELOPMENT

OBJECTIVES:

1. To increase vocabulary
2. To improve rapid automatic naming
3. To categorize
4. To understand and follow directions
5. To describe functions and features of objects

DESCRIPTION:

Choose a category related to a theme or current child interests. Ask children to name objects related to that category and list them. Have children refer to the list and then locate the objects and photograph them.

Print the pictures and mount each on a large index card. Share these photographs with the group, name what they are, discuss their uses, and describe their features. Challenge the class to name the pictures as quickly as possible.

Repeat the process with several other categories.

EXTENSIONS:

Small-Group Activities:

Glue one or more photographs from a category to a poster and label it. Put other photographs from that category on individual cards and laminate them. Repeat the process to make other category posters. Put out one category poster; stack face down the individual cards that belong in that category. Have one child act as the leader, turning over the top card and naming it before other group members do. The child who names it first earns the card. The person with the most cards wins.

To make the game more challenging, put out several category posters and corresponding object cards.

Independent Explorations:

The child sorts the object cards into categories by placing them next to the correct poster.

One-on-One Instruction:

Receptive Language: Sit with the child. Display individual object cards. Name one card and ask the child to hand it to you. Discuss the object's use.

Expressive Language: Hold all the photographs fanned out, facing you, as if playing cards. Ask the child to pick one card from your hand, to look at it, and to name and describe it.

Family Involvement:

Send a note home encouraging parents to go through categories of objects at home and to have their child name them and discuss their uses. For example, ask the parents to have their child name all the objects used to make dinner.

LANGUAGE CHECKLIST

	Baseline	Period 1	Period 2
Child: _____	__/__/__	__/__/__	__/__/__

Receptive Language

To listen carefully

To follow directions

To demonstrate an understanding of
  the meanings of words

To act out the meanings of new words

	Baseline	Period 1	Period 2

Expressive Language

To engage in dialogue, expressing oneself

To expand vocabulary

To use question words and forms correctly

To use new vocabulary appropriately in conversation

	Baseline	Period 1	Period 2

Action Words (Verbs)

To act out physically the meanings of verbs

To follow directions using action words

To identify named verbs in pictures

To describe actions in pictures

	Baseline	Period 1	Period 2

Position Words

To place objects in named positions

To name positions of objects

To point to positions of objects in pictures

To name positions of objects in pictures

To match pictures of objects by their positions

	Baseline	Period 1	Period 2

Descriptive Words

To identify people or objects by verbal descriptions

To describe physical attributes of people or objects

To explain the functions of objects

	Baseline	Period 1	Period 2

	Baseline	Period 1	Period 2
Child: _____	__/__/__	__/__/__	__/__/__

Labeling Objects

To match three-dimensional objects
To match photographs to their objects
To match photographed objects
To name three-dimensional objects
To name photographed objects

Verb Tense

To develop an appreciation for the passage of time
To sequence events in order of occurrence
To use regular past tense verbs correctly
To use irregular past tense verbs correctly
To use present tense correctly
To use future tense correctly

Possessive Words

To identify the ownership of objects
To use possessive words correctly

Color Words

To identify objects of a particular color
To name objects of a particular color
To name photographs of a particular color
To group photographs by color

CODE:
✔ = Does Consistently
± = Does Sometimes
✗ = Does Rarely/Does Not Do

$\mathcal{2}$

STORYTELLING/DRAMA

STORYTELLING/DRAMA INTRODUCTION

What Are Storytelling and Drama?

Storytelling is the age-old process of relating a tale based on a real-life event, fantasy, or fable. Oral history has been a way to transmit the shared experiences and expectations of a culture or group of people since long before written records. *Drama* is the act of portraying a story through actions and dialogue. Long before children perform in the school play, they pretend to be daddies, doctors, or superheroes.

Why Are Storytelling and Drama Important?

Storytelling is a way to transmit knowledge from one generation to another orally. It is also a method for teachers to engage young children linguistically, embedding concepts, vocabulary, and values in an interesting tale. The storyteller spins a yarn that requires the child to use imagination and to draw mental pictures. It is a valuable tool through which to model rich language.

Young children love to pretend. They easily assume the traits of another person, an animal, or an object. Through drama, children are able to say and do things that might not be acceptable in their personal relationships or daily lives. They can be brave when they don't feel brave, be naughty when they know that's not right, and be the boss when they know they are still too young to be in charge.

Dramatic play encourages children to negotiate the plot and to determine the needed characters with other children, to decide on the direction of the action, and to determine the types of props that might be needed. Through this, children plan, listen, express, socialize, negotiate, fight, and make up.

Dramatic play is a vehicle for young children to act out their understanding of a story, either real or made-up, as well as their understanding of the world in which they live.

How Are Storytelling and Drama Learned?

Storytelling is learned by being told stories frequently and by being encouraged to tell them. Children are exposed to storytelling very early in their lives. Mothers begin this with the little tales of Patty-Cake and This Little Piggy and sing the story "Rock-a-Bye Baby." Toddlers enjoy stories about other small children and revel when the storyteller is able to put them or their namesakes into the plot. Preschoolers enjoy hearing familiar stories told and retold and often join in.

Effective storytelling with young children includes the use of actions, changes of voices, props, and motions.

How Are Storytelling and Drama Facilitated?

Once a story has been told, there are many ways to encourage its retelling. The following are a few techniques for storytelling with young children:

- Show the cover of a book that has been read to the children many times. Use it as the focal point to hold the attention of the group. Instead of reading the book, tell the story in your own words.
- Display one or more key objects from the story and feature them during the appropriate point of retelling.
- Involve a puppet in the storytelling and relate the tale through this character.
- Create flannel board or magnetic board characters from this tale.
- Make masks or headbands for the children to wear during the storytelling and have the children participate at appropriate points.
- Create motions or sounds the children can make or do to enhance the plot and to keep them involved.

The idea of dramatic representation is learned by seeing teachers and parents assume voices and act out parts of a story. It is effected by using one object to represent another or by pretending to be someone or something else. Dramatic play develops naturally during the preschool years. It is facilitated by providing the time and environment that supports it.

Drama can be stimulated by providing a few simple props or costumes and by encouraging children to assume a role and to playact for a little while. Nursery rhymes are a simple place to begin. They are very short stories with simple plots, little dialogue, and identifiable characters. Children who are not acting out the story can participate by becoming members of the chorus that recites the rhyme as the action progresses.

I AM THE STORY

SKILL: DRAMATIC PLAY AND STORY RETELLING

OBJECTIVES:

1. To recall a story that has been read or told in enough detail to act it out
2. To act out the story
3. To create needed props and costumes
4. To describe the action of the story
5. To participate in the dialogue of the story where appropriate

DESCRIPTION:

After a familiar story has been told to the group, work with the children to assemble the props and costumes they need to act it out. Allow them to dramatize the story as it was originally told or to make up their own variations. Nursery rhymes and simple folk-tales make very good material for beginning dramatization. Take photographs as the drama is acted out.

Review the photos with the children and select those that most accurately depict the sequence of action. Use the photos to stimulate discussion of what is going on in each shot and where it belongs in the flow of the story. Once the group agrees on which photographs to include, mount the photos on cardboard. Attach felt or sandpaper to the back and put the picture cards into an envelope.

Show the cards to the group and demonstrate how the cards can be used on the flannel board to re-create the dramatization.

EXTENSIONS:

Small-Group Activities:

Explain that two or three children may work together, talking about the photographs in the envelope and deciding on the correct sequence of events. They then are to place the cards in sequence from left to right on a flannel board.

Independent Explorations:

Make one set of story-retelling cards for each dramatic play episode. Label each envelope so that children are able to identify its contents. Put these envelopes near a flannel board for use during free-choice time.

One-on-One Instruction:

Receptive Language: Place several photographs from the drama on the table in front of the child. Describe one of the pictures and ask the child to find it. For example, say, "Find Humpty Dumpty sitting on a wall."

Expressive Language: Print a second set of pictures. As you work with individual children, point to a photograph and have the child describe it. Write the child's description on the page, below the photograph. Talk with the child about the picture.

Family Involvement:

Make a set of story-retelling cards to send home. Place it in a thin box that has been covered with felt and can serve as a portable flannel board. Have the child share the story with a family member.

STORYTIME PUZZLE

SKILL: DRAMATIC PLAY AND STORY RETELLING

OBJECTIVES:

1. To act out a familiar tale
2. To recognize photographs of oneself and fellow students in costume
3. To identify photographs of props used in the reenactment
4. To describe each key picture depicting the drama

DESCRIPTION:

After reading a story or telling a tale, encourage children to act it out. Help them think of props or costumes they need. Let them take the lead in re-creating the story but assist them when the action stalls or when they need help with a transition. As the children depict their interpretation of the story, take photographs.

Enlarge and print key photographs. Be sure to capture each character, the main props, and dramatic interactions. Glue the pictures onto a large sheet of poster board or construction paper. Laminate each sheet and show it to the group. Discuss what is pictured. Then, as the children watch, cut the sheets into large puzzle-shaped pieces. Begin with only two or three pieces per picture and increase the number as the children become more skilled at puzzle assembly. Put together the puzzle as the group looks on and tell them that they may select these puzzles during center time.

EXTENSIONS:

Small-Group Activities:

Show the children how to mix up the pieces, choose one, and describe what is pictured (e.g., "I see the queen's crown."). Select subsequent pieces, describing what is pictured and then assembling the puzzle. When the puzzle is completed, the group should have covered all the main elements of the story.

Independent Explorations:

Put the pieces into a large envelope. Label it with pictures and words so that children can retrieve it and play with the puzzle during periods of free choice.

One-on-One Instruction:

Receptive Language: Place two or more puzzle pieces in front of the child. Name one of the objects in the photographs and ask the child to point to it.

Expressive Language: Turn all the puzzle pieces face down on the table. Challenge the child to pick one and to describe what is pictured on the other side. Once each piece has been described, the child may fit the pieces together.

Family Involvement:

Send the puzzle sets home for the child to play with family members. Include on the envelope directions to the parent, asking the child to describe each picture.

THE GREAT, MAGNETIC ME

SKILL: DRAMATIC PLAY AND STORY RETELLING

OBJECTIVES:

1. To use photographs mounted with magnetized tape to tell stories
2. To describe the people and events that occur in each photograph

DESCRIPTION:

Snap photographs of a child taking part in spontaneous, imaginative, pretend play. Be sure to capture any relevant props, costumes, or scenery to enhance the quality of the photos and to stimulate story retelling.

Print the digitized photographs; then mount and back them with magnetic tape. Attach the pictures to a magnetized board.

Share the pictures with the group. Show them how to use the materials; ask the child whose pictures are being displayed to describe what was occurring.

EXTENSIONS:

Small-Group Activities:

Distribute picture cards to group members at random to be organized in some order that describes their play or to create a new story.

Independent Explorations:

Place the materials and the magnetic board in a center with a tape recorder. Encourage the children to insert a blank cassette tape, describe the photographs, and play back what has been said.

One-on-One Instruction:

Receptive Language: Put all the magnetized photographs on the board and play an I'm Thinking Of . . . game. Say, "I'm thinking of," and then describe one of the pictures in detail. Keep adding more information until the child guesses which picture is being described.

Expressive Language: Help the child use the photographs as prompts to retell the story of her or his dramatic play.

Family Involvement:

Have the child take home the set of magnetized photographs, a small cassette tape player, and the tape that was recorded during "Independent Explorations" to share with parents and other family members.

CREATE-A-TALE

SKILL: STORYTELLING

OBJECTIVES:

1. To create a story from real-life events
2. To expand vocabulary and verbal expressive skills
3. To listen carefully to story segments previously created in order to add meaning to them

DESCRIPTION:

During any learning experiences, take photographs of the people, places, and things seen. Return to class and print the pictures.

Distribute the pictures to the class at random. Begin a story created by the group, in which different children describe the pictures in their possession at various times in the story. For example:

Once upon a time, we went on a trip to the _____ [name the place; the child who has that picture holds it up]. This place was very _____ [the child describes the building]. When we went inside, we met _____ [name a person and have the child with that picture hold it up]. She (or he) was a _____, who said, "_____." Then, . . .

Suggest to the children that they are free to volunteer any verbal description of their particular picture they choose. Tape record the story as it is being created.

EXTENSIONS:

Small-Group Activities:

Suggest that children look at the pictures and identify the sequence of events as they actually occurred. They then can put the photographs in that sequence.

Independent Explorations:

Allow the children to play the audiotape made during group time, placing the pictures into a pocket chart in the order described in the story.

One-on-One Instruction:

Receptive Language: Display all the pictures so that the child can see them and retell the story. Pause periodically, having the child locate the photograph of the person, place, or object that fits that portion of the plot.

Expressive Language: Use the same cards and the technique described above to work with a single child to elicit language. Recite the structure of a story, and each time a response is called for, encourage the child to describe the person, place, or thing in detail. Record the story so that the child can listen to it later.

Family Involvement:

Send home the individual story and its audiotape created during "One-on-One Instruction." Include the pictures and the story outline in a packet along with directions for parents on how to use the materials. Encourage the parents to use these materials to foster verbal expression and creativity in their child. This basic exchange could be done verbally with the child in the car, while waiting to pick up a sibling, or when simply enjoying each other's company.

TELL ME A TALE

SKILL: STORYTELLING

OBJECTIVES:

1. To create a story based on randomly selected pictures
2. To use imagination

DESCRIPTION:

Take a variety of photographs inside and outside the classroom. Print them and mount them on tagboard. Make sets of six to eight pictures, including in each set a location shot, some people, and some objects. Also make some tagboard strips with a descriptive term on each (e.g., *strangest, most wonderful, funniest*).

Tell the children they are going to look at some pictures that may not go together. Tell the children they are to use their imaginations and think up a story based on pictures they randomly select.

Some groups may need help getting started. Offer an introduction. For example:

One day, at the _____ [find the location card] I saw the _____ [description card] thing happen. I saw a(n) _____ [object or person card] and _____.

EXTENSIONS:

Small-Group Activities:

Use the same technique in a small group. Record their story and print it out to be read to the whole class later.

Independent Explorations:

Some groups may need help getting started. Make a chart on poster board with blank spaces for photographs to be added during the storytelling. This can be used as the story starter. For example, place the storytelling chart and photograph cards in the activity center with a tape recorder and blank tapes. Each child may insert a blank cassette and record one or more stories.

One-on-One Instruction:

Receptive Language: Display the pictures and make up a tale. As you describe each picture, pause briefly and ask the child to locate it. Then continue with the story.

Expressive Language: Begin a story and use the pictures as prompts. Encourage the child to create an appropriate description for each break in the tale. Record the story so that it can be replayed to the child later. Transcribe it on the computer and import the relevant photographs. Collect each child's stories and audiotapes so that they may be replayed and reread.

Family Involvement:

Play for parents the audiotape created by their child in the one-on-one session of the story. Encourage the parents to cut out random pictures from magazines and catalogs and to challenge their child to make up a story for those pictures.

BLOCK HEADS

SKILL: BLOCK PLAY

OBJECTIVES:

1. To engage in creative block play
2. To develop dramatic play skills
3. To enhance ability to create a story

DESCRIPTION:

Make personalized blocks to build on the children's desire to play with blocks. Take a digitized photograph of each child, laminate all the photographs, and then attach each picture to a unit block. Children can then put themselves into vehicles, drive up to their block structures, get out, and enter the buildings they have created. In this process, the children have the opportunity to develop a story line and to use their imaginations.

EXTENSIONS:

Small-Group Activities:

Periodically add photo blocks of people and objects that will enhance the play. For example, after a trip to the fire station, add several photo blocks of the firefighters the children have just visited.

Independent Explorations:

Individuals may choose to play alone, selecting the size and number of blocks and the personalized blocks to be included in their independent play.

One-on-One Instruction:

Receptive Language: Work on position words and other relevant vocabulary by giving the child one of the picture blocks and a direction to follow; for example, "Walk Jennifer all around your building. Put Jason in the bedroom."

Expressive Language: Engage in a dialogue with the child as you play together with the blocks. Encourage descriptions of movement of the photo block through the structures that have been built.

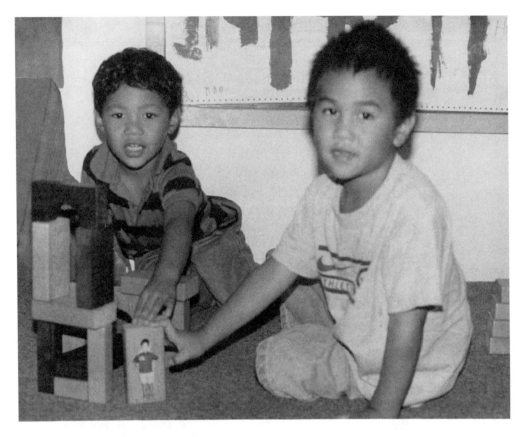

Family Involvement:

Send home copies of the photographs being used for picture blocks in school. Encourage child and parents to work together to make a set of homemade blocks from quart and half-gallon milk cartons. Provide directions on how to fold in the tops of milk cartons to form blocks. The cartons may be spray painted or left in their original form. The photographs may be added to some of these blocks.

MY OWN SLIDE SHOW

SKILL: DRAMATIC PLAY AND STORYTELLING

OBJECTIVES:

1. To dress in costumes
2. To work cooperatively to decide what the characters will be doing in these costumes
3. To view photographs of children in costumes and put them in some order according to the story line that has been developed
4. To add comments for each picture

DESCRIPTION:

Put out several costumes that suggest a theme of play. These can be occupation outfits, authentic ethnic costumes, or a variety of real-life outfits and props. Have the children interested in dramatic play put on the costumes; watch as spontaneous play occurs. Take a variety of candid photographs as the action progresses.

After the materials have been put away, process the photographs. Print them and talk with the children about what was happening in each one. Have the group sequence the pictures.

Take the group to the computer and import the digitized photographs into a slide show program. Put the pictures into the program in the sequence determined by the children. Add either text or the children's own recorded voices to the show.

Play the program for parents as they pick up their children from school.

EXTENSIONS:

Small-Group Activities:

Because this activity is a popular one, make it a regular activity choice for small groups.

Independent Explorations:

Print two hard copies of the photographs. Glue one set onto a sheet of construction paper to make a lotto board. Glue the second set onto individual cards that will fit onto each section on the lotto board. Show the game board and how to stack the cards and turn over the top card. The children can then match the pictures.

One-on-One Instruction:

Receptive Language: Use the photo cards made for the lotto game. Lay out a few pictures and describe a card. Have the child find that card and then affirm the selection in words. For example, say, "Yes, you found the picture of the fire hose."

Expressive Language: Play the slide show with the child; make sure that any sound effects or narrative that has been created is turned off. Have the child provide the description of what is happening in each picture.

Family Involvement:

Print a hard copy of the slide show and assemble it into a booklet to be sent home each night with a different child. Include a parent comment page. Ask each family to send it back with a brief comment.

WHEN I GROW UP

SKILL: STORYTELLING

OBJECTIVES:

1. To engage in dramatic play
2. To explore a variety of adult roles

DESCRIPTION:

Use digitized photographs of children to put them into a variety of real-life roles.

Take a close-up shot of each child. Scan a variety of photographs or illustrations depicting adults in their work clothes or uniforms. Crop each child photograph into an oval shape around the child's head. Cut out this digitized picture and move it into a scanned picture of an adult in her or his work clothes or uniform so that the child's head covers the adult's face in the original picture.

Repeat this process with each occupation being explored. Print a hard copy of each picture and assemble them into a "What I'd Like to Be" book.

EXTENSIONS:

Small-Group Activities:

Make a hard copy of each altered picture. Work with small groups to make occupations posters or booklets.

Independent Explorations:

Let the children look through magazines and coloring books to find scenes into which they would like to have their photographs imported.

One-on-One Instruction:

Receptive Language: Display the photographs of several children dressed in a variety of costumes. Describe one of the pictures and ask the child to find it; for example, "Where is the picture of James dressed as a baker?"

Expressive Language: Display the occupations posters and have the child talk about what is seen.

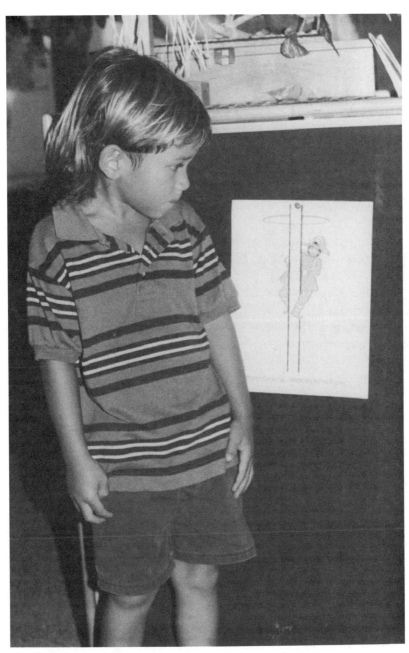

Family Involvement:

Send home several small head shots of the child. Ask the parents and child to look through magazines, cut out pictures of workers, and glue the pictures of the child's face onto the pages. Encourage the family to talk about what the child would be doing as a grown-up involved in this occupation.

PUPPET FUN

SKILL: STORYTELLING AND DRAMATIC PLAY

OBJECTIVES:

1. To make simple stick puppets
2. To create a story using the puppets

DESCRIPTION:

Take photographs of objects and people that relate to a theme or concept. Print each of these photos. Show the children how to mount them on construction paper and then attach each one to a craft stick.

Once the stick puppets are complete, have the group work cooperatively to create a spontaneous plot.

Videotape some of these story lines. All the actors will enjoy seeing their "opening night" over and over again.

EXTENSIONS:

Small-Group Activities:

Put sets of theme-related puppets the children have made into clear plastic bags. Display the puppets in the dramatic play area and encourage small groups to use them to develop their own little dramas.

Independent Explorations:

Provide candid photographs and miscellaneous magazines for children to cut apart to create individualized puppets. Encourage storytelling and dramatization.

One-on-One Instruction:

Receptive Language: Stick all the child-made stick puppets into a large block of Styrofoam. Have the child sit facing the display of puppets. Name or describe one and have the child select it and demonstrate something about it. For example, if the boy selects a frog, he may frog leap.

Expressive Language: Select one puppet and have the child select one or two for her- or himself. Start a dialogue in character and encourage the child to talk through one of the puppets.

Family Involvement:

Play the videotape for parents at a family event or show a short segment when they come to pick up their children at the end of the day. Send home a duplicate set of puppets for child and parents to play with briefly together.

WATCH ME

SKILL: DRAMATIC PLAY

OBJECTIVES:

1. To participate appropriately with props and costumes in beginning levels of dramatic play
2. To identify oneself in photographs taken during dramatic play
3. To comment verbally on pictures of oneself involved in dramatic play

DESCRIPTION:

Toddlers and young preschoolers enjoy dramatic play topics similar to their own experiences. Involve them with real objects and costumes and encourage simple play. They enjoy feeding the baby, being Mommy who carries the purse, being Daddy who drives the car, and pretending to talk on the telephone. Take photographs of the children as they take part in these activities.

Older preschoolers, kindergartners, and lower elementary school children like both fantasy play and more elaborate real-life reenactments. Their themes extend out of the home and into their neighborhoods and schools.

Print each of the photos and show them to the children. Have each child pick out a picture of her- or himself. Encourage the children to talk about what they see. Revisiting the experience this way reinforces the experience of the firsthand play.

EXTENSIONS:

Small-Group Activities:

Select one of the pictures, have one of the children describe what is happening in the picture, and then ask the whole group to pretend to do the same thing; for example, "Look. Molly is pretending to be Mommy sweeping with the broom. Let's all stand up and pretend to sweep."

Independent Explorations:

Enlarge the digitized photographs and make a photo gallery at the children's height along a wall that is accessible. Identify children who are between activities and seem to be having difficulty deciding what to do next; encourage them to go to look at a particular picture.

One-on-One Instruction:

Receptive Language: Make a set of pictures of each child you will work with on a one-on-one basis. Take the pictures out one at a time and comment on each one. Then lay the pictures on the table and have the child point to each one as you describe it.

Expressive Language: Put each of the child's pictures into a mini photo album. Sit with the child and ask her to tell you about the photographs.

Family Involvement:

Send the individualized photo albums home overnight with the children to share with their families. When the parents arrive at the end of the day, encourage them to sit with their child for a few minutes to look through their child's album. Have the child talk about what he was doing during playtime.

STORYTELLING/DRAMA CHECKLIST

	Baseline	Period 1	Period 2
Child: _____	_/_/_	_/_/_	_/_/_

	Baseline	Period 1	Period 2
To recall characters and plot of a story			
To act out a story			
To depict characters			
To use props and costumes appropriately			
To include dialogue in story reenactment			
To recognize costumed self in photographs			
To describe a scene in dramatic play photographs			
To retell a story, using dramatic play photographs			
To sequence a story, using dramatic play photographs			
To create a story from real-life events			
To create a made-up story			
To add to a story once started			
To engage in independent dramatic play			
To work cooperatively with others in dramatic play			
To explore a variety of adult roles			
To make stick puppets			
To create a story using puppets			

CODE:
✔ = Does Consistently
± = Does Sometimes
× = Does Rarely/Does Not Do

3

EMERGING LITERACY

EMERGING LITERACY INTRODUCTION

What Is Emerging Literacy?

There is no one point in an individual's life when the person suddenly becomes fully literate. Reading and writing are complex tasks built upon a variety of skills that evolve gradually over time.

Emerging literacy is the process of acquiring the foundation needed to learn how to read and write. It begins at birth and continues to the stage at which the child is able to employ basic, conventional reading and writing skills.

How Does Literacy "Emerge"?

Literacy builds upon the linguistic base of listening and speaking. Young children take in the language spoken to them and later experiment with the sounds and rhythms of that native language. These are the words they will later read and write. Development of solid receptive and expressive language is crucial to the process of becoming literate.

Recent research in emerging literacy reveals that young children do not enter kindergarten as blank slates, knowing nothing about either the reading or the writing process. They have, after all, lived in a literate culture, seeing the important people in their lives read newspapers, look up numbers in a telephone directory, consult signs, write checks, and jot down notes. These and many other everyday experiences have shown children that reading and writing are important and highly valued skills. Young children who see adults model the skills of reading and writing and who have been read to will eventually try to emulate these abilities and incorporate them into their dramatic play.

As they do with language, young children play with literacy and along the way develop a mental construct that helps them understand their experiences with print. A baby's first attempts to communicate come out as babble, an essential stage of language development. A young child's first attempts to write are expressed as scribble, an equally important stage in the development of both writing and drawing.

Young children explore and experiment with the materials of reading and writing. As they do with other early toys, infants hold, mouth, turn, throw, and look at their baby books to discover how these objects work.

Around the first birthday, children begin to develop an awareness that books are distinguished from their other toys, with a special purpose. They show a developing understanding of what is known as the conventions of reading by holding the book upright, looking at the pictures, and turning the pages. Preschoolers also begin to notice the logos for favorite products, environmental symbols such as stop signs, and the difference between the words *men* and *women* in public rest rooms.

About the same time that appropriate book behavior begins to develop, children start to explore the wonders of pencils, chalk, crayons, and marking pens. They discover that writing is the process of leaving permanent marks. Over time, the scribble begins to take on a more letterlike quality until finally actual letters emerge.

Finally, children who have been read to frequently develop a sense of written language. They become familiar with book language and begin to incorporate these words and language structures into their own oral language and into their play. Such a child may be seen holding a teddy bear in his lap as he "reads" the words "Once upon a time . . ."

Why Is Emerging Literacy Important?

The stages of development that precede formal reading and writing are crucial to the eventual mastery of these skills. They are as vital to the literacy process as learning to sit up and to pull oneself to standing are to learning to walk. Without these fundamental skills, formal reading and writing instruction is fruitless.

Young children must learn through early exposure to reading that the printed word is talk written down, that it is permanent, and that it can be read by others at any time. They need to understand that symbols represent real objects or concepts and that these symbols convey meaning. A frequent question soon becomes, "What does it say?"

Children must also learn that reading and writing are crucial skills to life in a modern world. They benefit from seeing parents and teachers read directions to a recipe, follow instructions to a new game, or jot down a note to a friend.

How Is Emerging Literacy Facilitated?

Early literacy is stimulated by providing a print-rich environment where reading and writing are an integral part of all activities. This can be accomplished in many ways. For example:

- Make a variety of fiction and nonfiction books available and use them frequently
- Label shelves and objects in the environment, fill the room with books, and use reference materials to look up answers to the children's questions
- Model reading and writing throughout the day yourself and introduce literacy props when appropriate in dramatic play
- Incorporate a writing center and stock it with materials that invite young illustrators and authors to express themselves
- Act as a secretary when a child wants to dictate a thought and have it recorded on paper
- Develop simple parent-child activity materials that can be sent home with a child or suggested to the parent to encourage literacy in the home

PICTURE A WORD

SKILL: EMERGING LITERACY—READING

OBJECTIVES:

1. To name a pictured object
2. To associate a pictured object with its spoken word
3. To associate a pictured object and its spoken word with its corresponding written word
4. To match three-dimensional letters with their printed form

DESCRIPTION:

Ask individual children to pick out one to four objects they would like to capture photographically. Depending on the age and skill level of the children, either take the photographs yourself or assist the children in framing and taking the shots. (Note: Select objects whose names have eight or fewer letters.)

Set up a page layout program so that a standard $8\frac{1}{2} \times 11$-inch page is divided in half horizontally. Insert one photograph into the top section and a second into the bottom.

Beneath each photograph, make a long, rectangular box. It will become the frame for individual letters that represent the name of the pictured object. Divide the frame into small boxes by inserting vertical strokes so that the number of small boxes equals the number of letters in the object's word.

Cut the page in half and mount it on construction paper. Add a frame of letters without the picture to the back. Laminate each card.

Provide a basket of plastic letters and show the class how to look for a specific letter. When you find the letter you want, place it in the frame over its matching letter and repeat the process until the word it completed. Then read the word aloud to the group.

EXTENSIONS:

Small-Group Activities:

To encourage cooperation, have children work in pairs to find the needed letters to form their word. Each pair may try to "beat the clock" by completing their word before the sand in an egg timer runs out.

Independent Explorations:

Each child can decorate a small shoe box, write his or her name on it, and store the cards created in this My Word Bank box.

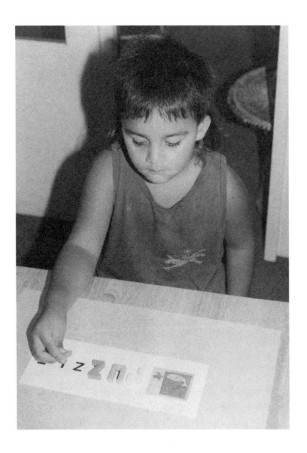

One-on-One Instruction:

Ask the child to pick one of the words from the box and to read it to you. Then name the letters to "spell" the word. As the child becomes more familiar with the words in the word bank, he or she turns the card over to read the side with the word only. The child can self-check by turning the card over to see the corresponding photograph.

Family Involvement:

Place a set of inexpensive plastic letters into the child's word bank box and secure with a rubber band. Send it home with a set of instructions for parents on how to match the letters and a note on the importance of encouraging their child's exploration of letters and sounds.

Make a parent-child activity by providing blank game cards and a computer-generated set of letter chips to be cut out. Include directions for the parent and child to look through old magazines, catalogs, or newspapers to find a picture to cut out and paste on the game board. Have the parent write the word in the letter frame, one letter per space. Then parent and child can cut out the letter cards and match them to the letters on the board.

MY FAVORITE CHARACTER

SKILL: EMERGING LITERACY—READING

OBJECTIVES:

1. To understand that print is talk written down
2. To become interested in the printed word by putting oneself into the story
3. To read one's own words

DESCRIPTION:

Have a child select a favorite book from the shelf of recently read storybooks and to pick a favorite character from that book. Ask the child to tell you what she likes about that character. Record what she says.

Provide props and materials for the child to make a simple costume, mask, or headband to represent the selected character.

Take a picture of the child in the costume she has made, holding the book so that the cover is visible.

Insert the picture into a page layout program and type in the dictated words describing the favored character. Print two copies—one to be sent home and one to be put into a page protector and added to the class book.

Share the book with the class at storytime and put it into the class library.

EXTENSIONS:

Small-Group Activities:

Have children work together to make costumes for all the characters from a book, legend, or fairy tale. Ask them to act out the story; document it with the camera. Later, print the photographs and have the children dictate or write captions to describe the story events in their own words.

Independent Explorations:

Encourage children to look through well-illustrated nursery rhyme books or children's books and then to create their own props or costumes with the variety of craft materials available. Provide a child-operated tape recorder and blank tapes for children to record their own words. When a child shows such initiative, offer to capture the moment on film and to transcribe the words.

One-on-One Instruction:

Read through the class book individually with the child, noting the conventions of Western reading—reading left to right, top to bottom, and from the front of the book to the back—and the written words.

Family Involvement:

Send home with the child a copy of the photograph and dictated words, encouraging parents to read their child's own words. Have them share the picture and caption with friends and other family members.

Encourage parents to look through family photographs with their child and to jot down what their child says about various pictures.

LABEL IT BOOK

SKILL: EMERGING LITERACY—READING

OBJECTIVES:

1. To label pictured objects
2. To understand the relationship between oral and written words
3. To read key words

DESCRIPTION:

As a young child's oral vocabulary increases, introduce the idea that words can be represented in print. Decide on a category of words to be explored. Work with a small group of children, having them identify objects that belong in that category. Take a photograph of each object named.

Print each photograph taken and label it in a large, bold, easy-to-read typeface.

Create a colorful cover and add a title that reflects the subject. For example, create *My Playground* or *Things at My New School* books.

Laminate the pages and cover, stack them, and bind them into a book. Share the book with the class and then place it in the class library to be explored independently.

Variation: For classes with children from bilingual or multilingual backgrounds, write the key word in all relevant languages.

EXTENSIONS:

Small-Group Activities:

Divide a large project into sections, having each small group work on one part of the whole. Tell them to make a *Label It* book section for the objects included in their portion of the project. After all the sections are completed, combine them and share the finished book with the whole class.

Independent Explorations:

Provide a variety of graphic material so that a child is able to cut or tear out a desired picture, glue it to paper, and then label it him- or herself or ask to have it labeled.

One-on-One Instruction:

Sit with individual children in the library corner as they go through the *Label It* book, reading the words.

Family Involvement:

Have children sign out various *Label It* books created by the class to share at home.

Parent and child might look through magazines or catalogs and make their own *Label It* book. For example, in the spring, they could look through seed catalogs to pick out desired plants and then make a *Label It* book entitled *Our Garden.*

PICTURE A PROJECT

SKILL: EMERGING LITERACY—READING

OBJECTIVES:

1. To associate pictures with words
2. To use words and pictures in a sequence
3. To use words and pictures to complete a project successfully

DESCRIPTION:

Identify an activity that requires a precise sequence of steps for the activity to be completed successfully—for example, making a mirror-image butterfly print. Take a photograph of each distinct step and print them all in a size that will fit on a sentence strip card. Write a brief description next to each photograph.

Place the completed sentence strips in a pocket chart.

Read each step, pointing to the words and then to the pictures before beginning the project. Tell the children that this project will be one of the options available for free choice. If they decide to do this project, they should simply follow the steps from the left side of the chart to the right side.

EXTENSIONS:

Small-Group Activities:

Take the strips out of the pocket chart, mix them up, and challenge a small group of children to reassemble them in the proper order by using both words and picture clues.

Independent Explorations:

Develop workjobs that can be done independently, with simple directions depicted in pictures and words.

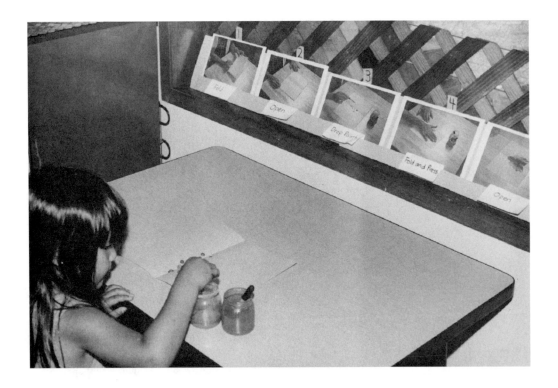

One-on-One Instruction:

Ask the child to describe the sequence of directions needed for the project to be completed, using the pictures and words as cues.

Family Involvement:

Develop parent-child activities with directions that can be depicted easily and quickly in pictures and words. Include the materials and the sheet of directions in a packet to be sent home.

LOOK AT WHAT WE DID

SKILL: EMERGING LITERACY—READING AND WRITING

OBJECTIVES:

1. To dictate a description of an activity
2. To read what has been written
3. To share printed words with others

DESCRIPTION:

Have the children recall a newly completed experience or activity. This would be an appropriate follow-up to the activity "Picture a Project." Record the children's descriptions of the activity on a large language experience chart. As you write, leave space to insert one of the photographs taken of the materials or during the experience.

After the group has come to a consensus about the events, take out a glue stick and distribute randomly the cut-out pictures to the class. Reread the story and, as you come to the space, have the child who has that picture come up and glue it onto the chart. Continue reading until the chart has been completed.

Fold the top of the chart over a hanger and staple it. Hang the story chart in the checkout area so that children are able to share it with their parents as they leave for the day.

EXTENSIONS:

Small-Group Activities:

Encourage groups of children to create their own language experience charts. When necessary, act as the secretary for the group or provide them with the spellings of words when requested.

Independent Explorations:

Mount all the language experience activities on hangers and hang them at child height in a spot where children can see and read them independently.

One-on-One Instruction:

Help each child make his or her own language experience pages to include in a personal journal.

Family Involvement:

Type the language experience chart story and insert the digitized pictures, reduced to letter-sized format, to send home with the child.

LOOK AT ME

SKILL: EMERGING LITERACY—WRITING

OBJECTIVES:

1. To express words and thoughts in writing
2. To see one's own words in print
3. To read one's own words to others

DESCRIPTION:

Ask a child to identify an activity at school that he finds particularly interesting. Take a photograph of him actively engaged in that activity.

Insert the picture into a page layout program on either a half or a whole page and either with or without lines, depending on the child's writing skills.

Invite the child to either write about what he is doing in the picture or dictate the description to an adult to transcribe. After this is completed, ask the child to share it with the class at group time. Repeat for each child in the class. Suggest that those who want to share sign up for a turn in the Author's Chair.

EXTENSIONS:

Small-Group Activities:

Children with common interests may choose to work on their projects together. This cooperative work requires children to communicate and negotiate to get an end product that pleases them all.

Independent Explorations:

Each child can assemble his or her collection of "Look at Me" activities into a scrapbook.

One-on-One Instruction:

Sit with the child as she writes; answer questions or provide written samples when asked for assistance.

Family Involvement:

Place the project into a plastic page protector and send it home with the child to share with family members as a favorite activity at school.

Encourage the parent to act as a scribe when the child dictates a short piece about a favorite activity at home.

GREETING CARDS

SKILL: EMERGING LITERACY—WRITING

OBJECTIVES:

1. To formulate thoughts to be expressed in writing
2. To observe one's own words being handwritten
3. To see one's own words in print or handwritten

DESCRIPTION:

Take a digitized photograph of each child or of the class as a whole. Insert the photo into the front of a card-making program.

Print a card for each child, to be used as a personalized greeting card, an invitation, or a thank-you note. Encourage the children to write or dictate messages and then to sign their cards.

Group cards can be used to acknowledge a class volunteer or to thank the host of a recent field trip. Have each child sign the card and add a short message or drawing.

Record on the card the thoughts of the younger children and have them sign it.

EXTENSIONS:

Small-Group Activities:

Form a small committee to create a message for the greeting card to be sent from the class.

Independent Explorations:

Print several copies of each card so that children have a ready supply of personalized greeting cards for their correspondence.

One-on-One Instruction:

Work with each child individually to create cards for parents for holidays, birthdays, Mother's Day, Father's Day, and special events. Assist the children by writing a model of the desired word for older children or by recording the younger children's words.

Family Involvement:

Ask parents to have family members send cards and letters to their young child. In return, they will need to help their child develop the habit of corresponding in response.

CATCH ME IF YOU CAN

SKILL: EMERGING LITERACY—WRITING

OBJECTIVES:

1. To write a description of one's actions and thoughts
2. To share one's written thoughts with others

DESCRIPTION:

Take candid photographs as the children work and play during the day. Insert each digitized photograph into a page layout program and print it. Make duplicates when more than one child is pictured.

Post the pictures in the writing center. Instruct the children to select picture sheets that feature their own pictures. Tell them to write a description of what they were doing as the picture was taken. Date the sheet and make a copy of it for the child's portfolio. Send the original home that day.

EXTENSIONS:

Small-Group Activities:

When several children are captured in a single photograph, have them work together to dictate an appropriate description of the activity.

Independent Explorations:

Make a file of extra picture sheets printed but selected by any child. Individuals may pick a picture at random to write about, using whatever level of written expression they are currently using. Provide a date stamp so that children can easily record the date of each composition.

One-on-One Instruction:

Take random photographs of the activity during the day and preview them with the child. Ask which photograph he would like printed. Encourage the child to write or dictate a description of what he was thinking, feeling, and doing as the picture was being taken.

Family Involvement:

Send home one of the pictures not selected for use during the day. Ask the child to tell the parent what was going on in the picture. Suggest that the parent write the words on the sheet. Encourage the youngster to bring the completed sheet back to school to share with the class as a written project that was completed with the parent.

As a special project, the parents may give their child a disposable camera to document their time together. When the pictures are developed, the parents can encourage their child to write about what is depicted in the photographs. The child may bring these to school to share with friends.

SAMPLE WORD CARDS

SKILL: EMERGING LITERACY—WRITING AND READING

OBJECTIVES:

1. To read key words
2. To identify letters and letter sequences
3. To copy letters from a sample

DESCRIPTION:

Emergent writers who are beginning to incorporate real letters into their writing often benefit from a model. Encourage these budding writing skills by providing a variety of blank writing cards that have pictured objects and a set of sample word cards that have the printed words completed. Laminate the sample cards. Encourage the children to look at the sample and to make their own sets of word cards.

When starting a new theme or area of interest, take some photographs of objects specific to that topic. For example, when exploring transportation, take photographs of a truck, a taxi, a train, and an ambulance.

After taking photographs of the desired objects, open a page layout program and orient it widthwise. Divide it in half to form two long cards. Insert one digitized picture along the left-hand edge of each section. Leave ample room for the child to write the name of the pictured object. Print several copies of each sheet and cut the pages in two to form individual writing cards.

Introduce the materials at group time. Show the children the blank picture cards and the laminated sample cards with the words. Let them know that this activity is available in the writing center. They may select one of each card, find the sample, and then copy the word onto their own sheets to take home.

EXTENSIONS:

Small-Group Activities:

Work with a small group to identify key words for an upcoming theme or unit. Have the group select the objects to be photographed for the new word cards. Depending on the skill and maturity level of the group, have them help take the photos. Then let this group of children be the first to try out the new set of completed cards.

Independent Explorations:

Provide some cards without pictures and a variety of old magazines and catalogs. The child can cut out desired pictures, glue them in place, and then write the words

independently. Date and save some of these efforts to add to the child's portfolio, comparing them with ones made from a model.

One-on-One Instruction:

Sit with one or two children briefly each day in the writing center as they work on their word cards. Observe their progress and note any problems they may be having.

Family Involvement:

Send home some blank cards and a laminated sample to be copied at home as the parents look on.

Send home blank word cards and ask the parents to identify words meaningful to parent-child activity. Ask the parents to write a word on one blank card as their child watches and then have the child copy it. The child may bring these special words cards to school to share with the class.

PERSONALIZED SHAPE BOOKS

SKILL: EMERGING LITERACY—WRITING

OBJECTIVES:

1. To express thoughts in writing
2. To experiment with written language
3. To collect written thoughts in a booklet

DESCRIPTION:

As the group explores a theme or project, take photographs. Print one copy of each photograph. Have the children look through the pictures and select those they would like to include in a personalized book. Then print the desired pages for each child.

Insert the selected pages into a large sheet of construction paper folded in half to form a cover. Staple along the edge. Add a precut shape that depicts the theme or topic of the pages; glue it to the front cover. For example, if the class has recently visited a farm and now has incubating chicken's eggs in class, make a cover shape of a chick that has recently pecked its way out of its shell.

Put these booklets in the writing center. Encourage children to spend time looking through their individualized materials and writing about the pictures they have chosen to include.

EXTENSIONS:

Small-Group Activities:

Work with a few children to make a group shape book. Have them determine the theme, select the pictures to be included, and help with making and decorating the cover and writing the individual pages.

Independent Explorations:

Once a child has completed the personalized shape book, provide additional pages the child may use for independent writing. In each, the photograph will stimulate the written expression.

One-on-One Instruction:

Work with individual children, helping them with their writing as requested or required. Observe each child's progress, noting anyone who regularly avoids writing ac-

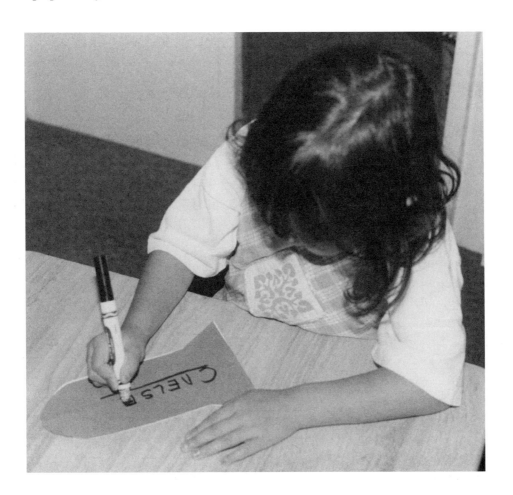

tivities or who seems to be having an unusual amount of difficulty with the physical skills of manipulating a pencil.

Family Involvement:

Send home the finished shape book for the child to read and share with family members. Encourage parents to be supportive of their child's efforts at written expression, even when not perfect by adult standards.

EMERGING LITERACY CHECKLIST

	Baseline	Period 1	Period 2
Child: _____	_/_/_	_/_/_	_/_/_

Reading

	Baseline	Period 1	Period 2
To observe people reading			
To show an interest in symbols			
To show an interest in print			
To ask to have words identified			
To ask to have stories read			
To understand the conventions of reading (left to right, top to bottom, front to back)			
To look at books independently			
To name pictured objects			
To add pictures to a rebus			
To discuss the characters and events in books			
To contribute to a language experience story			
To match three-dimensional to printed letters			
To match letters			
To rhyme words			
To listen for sounds in words			
To match letters and sounds			
To identify written letters			
To read one's own name			
To read key words			
To read words and sentences in a book			

Child: _____

Writing

To watch adult writers

To ask what an adult is writing

To ask to be read what has been written

To dictate words to be written by others

To write, although not legible by others

To copy letters

To form identifiable letters from memory

To copy one's own name

To write one's own name

To write individual words

To express thoughts and feelings in writing

To collect one's own writing in book form

CODE:
✔ = Does Consistently
± = Does Sometimes
✕ = Does Rarely/Does Not Do

4

SOCIAL STUDIES

SOCIAL STUDIES INTRODUCTION

What Is Social Studies?

Social studies involves the study of one's self in relationship to others and to the environment. It addresses human relationships and interdependence, from the immediate family to the global community. It explores the acquisition of social and cultural understanding through the study of current and historical topics.

Why Is Social Studies Important?

Every child is born with a unique identity, part of a family, neighborhood, ethnic group, culture, community, country, and world. She is a social being on a quest for relevance, striving to discover how she fits into the story of life. Social studies offers opportunities to develop an understanding and appreciation of similarities and differences in people, abilities, and preferences. Moreover, it teaches children about themselves and the choices to be made in becoming productive, responsible members of a community.

How Is Social Studies Learned?

Social studies begins with nurturing experiences that help children develop self-esteem, self-direction, and self-control. As children take responsibilities for classroom chores, choose from among a variety of learning activities, and participate in cooperative projects, they begin to develop a sense belonging. Through interactions with their peers and adults in school, they learn how to develop relationships and to see themselves as a part of a group or community, outside their own families.

Children gain a growing sense of how society works by learning about their ancestors through books, art, and artifacts and through visits and personal interactions with people of various occupations, professions, and businesses. They learn about technology as they use machines, tools, and the technology. They learn about other cultures and geography as they encounter people of different ethnic groups and share stories, food, music, games, customs, and traditional dress.

How Is Social Studies Facilitated?

To make social studies relevant for young children, educators must understand the child's world and link learning with family and community values and goals. By developing activities that provide meaningful, firsthand experiences, children begin to make important connections between themselves and others. These connections can be promoted in a wide variety of ways:

To foster a recognition and appreciation of human similarities and differences:

- Take and display photographs of the children and their families
- Use songs and games that spotlight individual characteristics, abilities, likes, and dislikes
- Invite children to share experiences, thoughts, and ideas
- Prominently display children's work in the classroom

To develop an understanding of family and community roles:

- Invite family members to visit the classroom to share life experiences, jobs, and talents
- Invite resource people and community helpers to visit the classroom and to talk about their work and share the tools of their trade
- Take children out into the community to visit stores, offices, factories, libraries, hospitals, fire stations, farms, and so on
- Participate in community events and celebrations

To develop an awareness, understanding, and appreciation of other cultures:

- Read the children books about other peoples and cultures
- Invite children's family members and others to share pictures, stories, artwork, songs and dances, artifacts, clothes, and food from different ethnic groups
- Provide a wide variety of costumes and props for integrating learning and for re-creating concepts through dramatic play
- Have the children prepare and eat ethnic foods

To promote an awareness of the relationship between people and the environment:

- Use maps and globes with the children when talking about familiar places or learning about new places
- Have the children plant and care for a garden that includes indigenous and foreign plants and crops
- Take excursions to nearby farms, gardens, forests, bodies of water, mountains, and so on

Children gain an understanding of rights and responsibilities and learn to become vital, productive members of the classroom community when they participate in directing their learning, planning their day, and caring for themselves, others, and the classroom environment. An awareness of human interdependence will emerge if teachers embed cooperative learning throughout the curriculum and provide opportunities for direct personal experiences with others in the community.

SHINING STARS BOOK

SKILL: SOCIAL STUDIES—PROSOCIAL BEHAVIOR

OBJECTIVES:

1. To gain self-esteem
2. To participate in positive peer interactions
3. To recognize positive traits such as sharing and empathy
4. To improve communication skills

DESCRIPTION:

Watch for prosocial behaviors from the children and take digital photographs of children engaged in those behaviors. Enlarge each photo to a 5 × 7-inch picture and print it.

Gather the children into a group and show them the photos. Invite children to identify the people pictured and to describe and discuss what is happening. Ask the children who are shown in the photos to describe their feelings. Record their comments on the paper, below the photo. Display the papers on a bulletin board.

Encourage children to look for and catch their classmates displaying a specific behavior. Explain that when they see someone _____ [e.g., helping], they should tell a teacher, who will then take a photograph of it. If the children are capable, they may take the photographs themselves.

Bind the papers together into a *Shining Stars* book.

EXTENSIONS:

Small-Group Activities:

Work with the children who are shown in the particular photographs. Ask both giver and receiver of the behavior to describe how the event felt to each one. Record their comments on the photograph page.

Independent Explorations:

Place the *Shining Stars* book in the classroom library. Put hand-shaped blank books on the writing table and encourage children to illustrate their own stories, depicting a time when they helped someone. After a child finishes her or his illustrations, the child may dictate the story.

One-on-One Instruction:

Describe to the child a specific prosocial behavior. Brainstorm with him some ways the behavior might be displayed. Give the child the digital camera and explain how to operate it. Instruct him to "catch" classmates showing that behavior and to take a photograph of it. Print out the photograph and have the photographer dictate why he chose to take the photograph and what prosocial behavior it displays.

Family Involvement:

Send home the *Shining Stars* book to share with parents. Invite the parents to recall specific ways their child showed this same behavior at home, to write it down, and to send it to school for their child to share with classmates.

WATCH ME GROW!

SKILL: SOCIAL STUDIES—SOCIAL-EMOTIONAL DEVELOPMENT AND SELF-AWARENESS

OBJECTIVES:

1. To develop an awareness of developing abilities
2. To develop an awareness of physical growth
3. To increase self-esteem

DESCRIPTION:

Prepare for this activity by asking parents to send several pictures of their child to school that show various stages of growth: newborn, sitting, crawling, walking, nursing or bottle feeding, parent feeding the baby, and baby feeding her- or himself.

Scan the family photographs and digitize them. Print two copies of each picture. Glue together three sheets of legal-sized paper and fold to make nine pages of an accordion-folded book.

Give the child one set of family photographs and talk about the pictures, helping the child sequence them in developmental order. Instruct the child to glue the pictures in order onto the accordion-folded pages of the book. Ask the child to describe the action; record her or his words under the picture.

Take photographs of each child, beginning with orientation to school and continuing, capturing social-emotional development for about 2 months.

Print two sets of photographs for each child and make an accordion book of sequential development as described above. Record children's comments about the photographs and how the children have changed as they have grown.

EXTENSIONS:

Small-Group Activities:

Invite two or three children to look at each other's accordion books and to comment about the growth they have seen in both their friends and themselves. Record comments about similarities and differences.

Place on the table several photographs depicting developmental milestones of each child. Describe a child at a certain developmental level. For example, say, "I am thinking of a boy who used to hold on to his mommy's legs every morning but who now just waves good-bye."

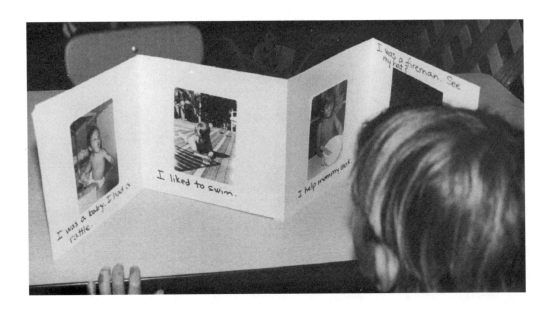

Independent Explorations:

Place the second set of photographs into a plastic bag and store in a file folder with the book. The child can sequence the set of pictures without looking at the book and then check for correctness by comparing the sequenced picture cards with the sequence in the accordion book.

One-on-One Instruction:

Place the set of the child's pictures on a table. Describe an ability or preference inferred by a specific photograph and ask the child to guess the photograph. For example, when looking at a photograph of the child building a block castle, say, "You used to just pile up blocks, but now you plan and build structures."

Family Involvement:

Send home the accordion book depicting the child's social-emotional development at school. Encourage the parents to read through it with their child, discussing the growth and their sense of pride in the child's accomplishments.

WHERE IN THE WORLD ARE WE?

SKILL: SOCIAL STUDIES—GEOGRAPHY

OBJECTIVES:

1. To develop geographical awareness
2. To develop an appreciation of other cultures
3. To gain an understanding of family members

DESCRIPTION:

Take head shots of each child and input those photographs into a wallpaper page that makes multiple copies of a photograph. Cut out the small wallpaper portraits to be used as stickers with a large U.S. map attached to a wall.

Send a note home asking parents, other family members, and family friends who are planning a trip within the United States to send postcards, souvenirs, or mementos of their travels to the child.

After the child receives and examines the items, the parent should name the city and state the items came from and help the child put them in a bag labeled with the location.

Ask the child to bring and share about the items at school, find the location on the U.S. map, and attach one of his or her photo stickers.

Keep the map up for the entire school year, noting how many places the children have visited without leaving home.

EXTENSIONS:

Small-Group Activities:

Place several objects made in different countries into a cloth bag. Let the children take turns reaching into the bag and picking an object. Help the child read where the object was made and try to find the location on a world map. Encourage the children to help each other read the names of the countries and to find them on the map.

Independent Explorations:

Make a classroom travel log containing the photographs described below. Use a three-ring binder to contain the pages and label a tab with each child's name. Place the binder in the class library or dramatic play area for individual children to peruse.

One-on-One Instruction:

Take digital photographs of each of the souvenirs as the children bring them in. Import each photo into a page layout program, label it with the city and state of origin, and print it out. For each photograph, ask the child to explain who sent the item and something about it. Record the response on the bottom of the page. Punch holes in the paper and place it in the appropriate section of the classroom travel log.

Family Involvement:

Send home a small paper bag, a line drawing of a world map, and a note asking parents to help their child find something with a label that tells where it was made (e.g., a cup labeled "Made in China"). Suggest that parents work with their child to find the country on the world map and to mark an X on the spot. Advise the parents to put the item back into the paper bag with the marked map and to send it to school with their child. At school, encourage the child to share the item during group time, show the label and name the country in which it was made, and then find the country on the classroom globe or world map.

CHEF DU JOUR

SKILL: SOCIAL STUDIES—MULTICULTURAL AWARENESS AND APPRECIATION

OBJECTIVES:

1. To discover and recall the ethnic groups represented in the class
2. To taste and compare foods from different cultures
3. To hear and learn words in several languages

DESCRIPTION:

Send notes home to parents, inviting them to come to class and prepare an ethnic recipe for a snack. Include a sign-up sheet with a choice of days and times.

When the visiting chef arrives, take a digital photograph of the person. Import the photo into a page layout program with the name of the chef, the name of the recipe, and the country in which it originated.

Take a series of four photographs as the chef prepares the food. Take another photograph of the children eating the food. Enlarge each photograph to 5 × 7 inches. Print out, seriate, and bind them together in a *Memory Book.*

Share the photographs with the children during group time. Show them the photo of the chef, read the person's name, the name of the recipe, and the country in which it originated. Locate the country on a world globe or map.

Ask the children to recall what the chef was doing in each photo; record their comments under each picture. Show the children the picture of them eating the food; record their comments about it.

As each new chef visits the classroom to share a recipe, take photographs as described above and add them to the *Memory Book.* Place the completed book in the library center for children to look at; invite parents to take turns borrowing the book.

EXTENSIONS:

Small-Group Activities:

Import the six photographs from each recipe (the one of the chef, the four of the preparation, and the one of the children eating) into a page layout program, making a game board with the first three pictures on the top row and the next three in the series on the bottom. Print two copies of the layout. Cut one layout into individual pieces, mount them on card stock, and laminate. Mount the game board on card stock and laminate. Invite children to choose a game board. Place the individual cards face down on the table and play a game using lotto rules.

Quesadillas

1. Place a flour tortilla on a plate.

2. Spread mild salsa on the tortilla with a spoon.

3. Sprinkle grated cheese on the salsa.

4. Cover with another tortilla.

5. Cook in a microwave oven for 30 seconds and serve.

Maria and her mother showing the class how to make quesadillas.

Independent Explorations:

Print out another set of game boards. Cut out the individual photographs and glue them onto index cards. Place them on a tray on a table so that children can sort the cards into ethnic recipes.

One-on-One Instruction:

Make recipe charts and invite the child to help prepare a specific recipe as a snack, recalling the country of origin and family member who shared it with the class.

Family Involvement:

Send home a set of picture cards from a recipe with a note instructing parents to help their child glue the cards to a sheet of paper, in order of occurrence. Suggest that the parents ask their child to describe the sequence of action taking place in each photo and then record their child's responses.

FACE THE FEELING

SKILL: SOCIAL STUDIES—EMOTIONS

OBJECTIVES:

1. To identify the four basic emotions: happy, sad, angry, scared
2. To relate feelings to facial expressions
3. To become aware of the physical manifestations of emotions

DESCRIPTION:

Discuss feelings and what situations elicit specific feelings. Sing "If You're Happy and You Know It," using facial expressions for happy, sad, angry, and scared. Take a digital head shot of each child expressing happiness and then sadness. Print a copy of each.

Cut or have children cut two 3-inch circles from tagboard. Glue the two circles together, sandwiching a craft stick between them. The result should look like a paddle.

Instruct the children to cut around their two head shots. Then have them glue the photograph showing a happy face to one side of the paddle and the sad face to the other side.

Invite the children to bring their emotions paddles to group time and to place them on the floor in front of them. Describe a scenario and ask a child to show you how it makes her feel by placing either the happy or sad photograph face up. For example, say, "You come home from school and Mom surprises you with your favorite ice cream."

As children progress in identifying emotions, add an angry/scared paddle. Encourage the children to use their emotions paddles to identify the feelings of characters in a story as you read it.

EXTENSIONS:

Small-Group Activities:

Make an emotions lotto game by importing the head shots of the children into a page layout program. Make four different lotto boards with three pictures on the top row and three on the bottom row. Make sure each board has pictures in a different order. Print out a second set of lotto boards, cutting the pictures apart and mounting them on card stock. Children can play Emotions Lotto by taking turns picking the top card from a stack and placing it over the matching picture.

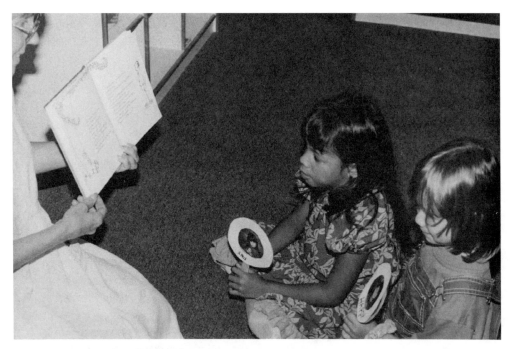

Independent Explorations:

Tape record yourself reading common statements with different emotions (e.g., "I'm hungry"). Pause between each reading. Children can play the tape and use emotions paddles to show how they think the speaker feels.

One-on-One Instruction:

Ask the child to choose a book to read. Tell the child that as you read the book aloud, he should use the emotions paddles depicting happy, sad, angry, and scared to show you how the characters in the book feel at specific times. Pause and talk about the reasons for the child's conclusion.

Family Involvement:

Print out on individual pages a second set of head shots for each child depicting happy, sad, angry, and scared. Send the four pages home with instructions for parents to talk with their child about each picture and what things make the child feel that way. Request that the parents record on the page what the child says and send it to school for the child to share.

MAPMAKERS

SKILL: SOCIAL STUDIES—GEOGRAPHICAL AWARENESS

OBJECTIVES:

1. To develop spatial awareness
2. To identify structures and landmarks in relation to the physical environment
3. To develop basic map-reading skills

DESCRIPTION:

Take digital photographs of doors, windows, furniture, fixtures, and large equipment in the classroom. Print copies. Cut out the objects from the pictures and laminate them. Glue a piece of felt to the back of each object picture. Cover a bulletin board with flannel fabric and use yarn to form the basic shape of the classroom.

During group time, give each child a felt-backed picture. Ask, "Who has a door?" Invite the children with the door pictures to come up and position the pictures on the classroom outline; give guidance when necessary. Ask for the windows next, proceeding in the same manner. Ask the children, one at a time, to identify their item, locate it in the classroom, and attach it to the corresponding place on the classroom map.

Take photographs of structures, landmarks, and plants on the playground and repeat the process described above to create a playground map.

EXTENSIONS:

Small-Group Activities:

Place the set of felt-backed pictures of classroom items on a tray by the flannel board. Encourage small groups of children to work together to affix the items pictured to the correct place on the classroom outline, creating a map.

Independent Explorations:

Place together all the felt-backed pictures from both the playground and the classroom. Children can sort the pictures into inside and outside items. They can choose to make either the classroom or playground map. Provide yarn for the map perimeter, and children can make the map by using the appropriate set of pictures.

One-on-One Instruction:

Using the felt-backed photographs of objects, take turns with the child in designing a different room. One person gives the instructions about where to place the objects, and the other person puts the picture of each object in the place indicated. For example, say, "Place a door in the upper left corner of the room."

Family Involvement:

Send home a note asking parents to walk through their home with their child, naming and counting the rooms. Ask the parents to draw the perimeter of the floor plan of their home and, working with their child, determine where each room and door should be located on the floor plan and then draw it in the appropriate place. Have them ask their child to name each room and write those words on the plan. Suggest that this plan can be used as an evacuation plan if arrows are drawn in that show the way out of the home in case of an emergency. Urge parents to post this plan and to practice evacuating the home.

WHAT'S IN HERE?

SKILL: SOCIAL STUDIES—COMMUNITY AWARENESS

OBJECTIVES:

1. To develop classification skills
2. To become aware of community stores and buildings
3. To match stores with their goods

DESCRIPTION:

Take the children on an excursion to the center of town or to a mall or on a walk around the neighborhood. Take photographs of the outside fronts of the buildings (including stores) and several objects commonly found inside the buildings (and stores). For the building photographs, enlarge the outside of each building to 8 × 10 inches. Print out all the photographs and laminate them.

Gather the group. Place the large pictures of the building fronts in a row across the floor, facing the children. Place the photographs of the objects into a decorative bag. Invite the children to come up in turn to pick a picture out of the bag, identify the picture, and place it under the building in which it is found.

EXTENSIONS:

Small-Group Activities:

Mount each large picture of the front of a building or store onto the upper part of 12-inch square poster board. Create a horizontal fold 2 inches from the bottom of the poster board to make a pocket. Place the photographs of the inside objects onto a tray. Invite small groups of children to work together to identify, sort, and put the object cards into the correct building pockets. Color-code the backs of the building pictures and their contents for self-correction.

Independent Explorations:

Place the building pocket poster boards and object pictures in the learning center for individual classifying.

One-on-One Instruction:

After using the photograph posters and cards, suggest classifying the contents of a building. Ask the child to recall other items she remembers seeing and write them down on individual cards. Invite the child to make an illustration for each item named and add them to the classifying game.

Family Involvement:

Send home an old store advertisement supplement or coupon booklet. Ask parents to help their child cut or tear items out and to make a collage of store departments by categorizing items and gluing them onto paper.

OCCUPATION VISITATION

SKILL: SOCIAL STUDIES—COMMUNITY WORKERS

OBJECTIVES:

1. To learn the names of several occupations and professions
2. To match tools and uniforms with corresponding jobs
3. To recall and describe the work involved in several jobs

DESCRIPTION:

Invite workers from the community to visit the classroom and share their occupation or profession with the children. Ask them to come clothed in what they wear at work and to bring in tools common to their trade. Prepare them to talk with the children in an age-appropriate way, using simple, concrete language. Request that they talk about their occupation and clothes and demonstrate how their tools are used. Allow the children to examine and use the tools if safe and appropriate.

Take individual digital photographs of each worker dressed in work clothes and of any clothing accessories and work tools. Input the photograph at the top of the page in a 4 × 6-inch frame and print it.

During group time, show each picture and ask the children to recall the name of the person, the name of the occupation, and the names of the tools. Ask the children to describe the job and to tell how the worker uses each tool. Record responses on the corresponding photo pages and bind them together in a three-pronged clear-covered portfolio to make a book. Use the picture of the worker as the cover page of the book. Repeat for each worker who visits the classroom.

EXTENSIONS:

Small-Group Activities:

Print a second set of photographs with labels under each picture. Cut out each picture and mount it on a 5 × 7-inch index card. Have each child pick a photograph of a different worker. Stack the tools-of-the-trade cards face down on a table. Let the children take turns picking the top card, identifying the tool, and giving it to the classmate with the corresponding worker picture.

Independent Explorations:

Place all the worker and tool cards on a tray on the floor. The child can group the workers with their appropriate tools.

One-on-One Instruction:

Gather the worker and tool picture cards. Show the child a picture of a worker and ask the child to name the occupation. Ask the child to recall the tools used in the occupation without looking at the pictures. Reveal the tool cards and let the child check to see whether he remembers them all. Ask the child to look at the tool cards and to describe how the tools are used.

Family Involvement:

Send home a note asking parents to talk with their child about their jobs, describing their work schedules and responsibilities. Suggest taking their child to the workplace. Invite parents to visit the classroom to share their jobs with the children. Make photographic records of their visits.

WHO'S PLAYING?

SKILL: SOCIAL STUDIES—MULTICULTURAL AWARENESS

OBJECTIVES:

1. To become aware of a variety of musical instruments from around the world
2. To match a person in ethnic dress with the corresponding musical instrument
3. To identify and name several ethnic musical instruments
4. To become aware of a variety of cultures and people

DESCRIPTION:

Invite musicians to make individual visits to the classroom and to play an instrument for the children. Locate instruments from various cultures. Tape-record the music.

Take three digital photographs of each visit: one of the musician playing the instrument, one of the musician alone, and one of the instrument alone. Print and mount the individual pictures on 4 × 6-inch index cards and laminate them.

Have the children listen to a piece of taped music and find the picture of the musical instrument being played. Pause the tape and name the instrument. Have the children identify the picture of the person playing the instrument and place the instrument and player pictures side by side. Continue playing the music and having children find the corresponding instrument and person.

After the children have matched all the instruments with the musicians, check for accuracy by showing the group the picture of the musician playing the instrument.

EXTENSIONS:

Small-Group Activities:

Put musical instruments and items of ethnic clothing in a learning center for children to explore. Take digital photographs of children wearing costumes and playing instruments. Print the pictures and display them in the learning center.

At the snack center, display a photo of a musician playing an instrument. Provide an ethnic snack from the instrument's country of origin.

Independent Explorations:

Place a variety of materials for making musical instruments in the art center. Include small boxes, rubber bands, cups, beans, tape, oatmeal boxes, empty toilet paper rolls, and so on. Children can make rhythm and stringed instruments.

One-on-One Instruction:

Play a guessing game with the child. Place all the instrument and musician picture cards face up on a table. Describe an instrument or musician. For example, say, "I'm thinking of an instrument that has four strings and comes from Hawaii." Ask the child to point to the correct picture and to name it. Take turns letting the child describe an instrument or musician.

Family Involvement:

Send home a photograph of the child playing a musical instrument (see "Small-Group Activities"). Instruct parents to ask their child to comment on playing the instrument and to talk about the experience. Suggest that the parents record their child's responses underneath the photograph and send it to school for their child to share with the class.

YOU MUST HAVE BEEN A BEAUTIFUL BABY

SKILL: LANGUAGE—VERBAL EXPRESSION

OBJECTIVES:

1. To match a young child with her or his baby picture
2. To share personal history
3. To improve verbal expressive skills
4. To build self-esteem

DESCRIPTION:

Prepare for this activity by requesting that each set of parents send a baby picture of their child to school. Inform them that good care will be taken of the photograph and that it will be returned the next day. Scan each picture and print and mount it. Also ask parents to write a few thoughts about their child as a baby (e.g., "On the day she was born . . ." or "The thing I remember most about him as a baby is . . ." or "The cutest thing my child ever did as a baby was . . .").

Take a close-up photograph of each child in the class, enlarge it, and print it on letter-sized paper. Have each child select a background paper and mount the photo on the paper.

Gather the group and place a random selection of current student photographs on a display board. Chat with the group about the pictures and then pose the following: "I wonder what these children looked like when they were babies. Look at this picture. Can you guess which child this was as a baby?" Encourage children to guess who the mystery baby is. Record their predictions on a chart.

Invite the child whose baby picture it is to come up. Have the group look at the predictions on the chart to see how many children correctly guessed who this "beautiful baby" is. Read to the group the comments the parents sent about this child as a baby. Stimulate a discussion among the children about what they have seen and heard.

EXTENSIONS:

Small-Group Activities:

Work with two or three children to mount their pictures in an *Our Class Baby Book*. Put the scanned photograph of the infant and the parents' words on one side of a magnetic page photo album. On the other side, put the child's current picture and information the child would like recorded. For example, "I am 43 inches tall and weigh 51 pounds. My favorite food is pizza. I like to draw and play at the water table."

Independent Explorations:

Put several baby pictures and current pictures in the learning center for discussion and matching. Place matching color dots on the backs of the pictures to make the activity self-correcting. For example, Sara's baby picture and current photograph each have a purple dot on the back.

One-on-One Instruction:

Place several current photographs of classmates on the table and describe them for the child. For example, say, "I am thinking of a child who has long red hair and who likes to play in the housekeeping center and paint at the easel."

Print a 4 × 6-inch photograph on a letter-sized page. Show the child her baby picture and record what she says about it. Read the child's own words aloud.

Family Involvement:

Send home the *Our Class Baby Book* each night with a different child. Encourage the parents to read through it with their child, discussing the different classmates and finding the child's own pages.

SOCIAL STUDIES CHECKLIST

	Baseline	Period 1	Period 2
Child: _____	_/_/_	_/_/_	_/_/_

Psychology

To develop positive self-esteem
To identify prosocial skills
To recognize positive social traits
To improve verbal communication
To become aware of growth and development
To identify basic emotions
To understand that all people have feelings
To understand that emotions affect people
  physically
To explore one's own personal history
To understand the relationship of self to others

Geography

To develop geographical awareness
To locate family and friends geographically
To develop basic map-reading skills
To identify structures and landmarks on a map

Multicultural Awareness

To develop awareness of one's own culture
To appreciate other cultures
To explore the food, dress, and customs of other cultures
To examine a variety of musical instruments and music

Community Awareness

To identify buildings in the community
To name common objects related to those buildings
To match goods with places of business
To name common community workers
To match tools and uniforms to occupations
To describe the type of work for each occupation

CODE: ✔ = Does Consistently   ± = Does Sometimes   × = Does Rarely/Does Not Do

5

PHYSICAL
DEVELOPMENT

PHYSICAL DEVELOPMENT INTRODUCTION

What Is Physical Development?

Physical development is the natural process of growth and maturation that occurs during childhood and adolescence. It includes large and small muscle skills and balance. An individual changes from a helpless infant unable to direct or control voluntary movement to a physically strong and agile teen capable of playing Mozart, sinking a 20-foot jump shot, or using tweezers to remove a splinter.

Physical skills include muscle strength, agility, control, coordination, flexibility, stamina, and balance. Physical competence is achieved when the child is able to control and care for his or her body and to perform tasks at the desired level of proficiency.

Why Is Physical Development Important?

Children explore their world through movement. Those with limited mobility because of physical disabilities are challenged in the exploration of their environment and in all the learning this investigation provides. Young children are active learners propelled by their mobility.

Reaching a motor milestone is an important achievement for both the young child and the parents. These milestones are highly visible signs of the growth and development the child is experiencing. Physical competency represents important developmental objectives during the early years and leads to a sense of achievement and self-confidence.

How Is Physical Development Learned?

Physical growth and development follow a predictable sequence, progressing gradually over time and with experience from the head and traveling downward and from the center of the body out to the extremities. Large muscle strength and coordination precede small muscle control. Physical development requires repeated opportunities to move, using muscles and experimenting with balance.

Physical development has its own timetable and cannot be rushed. Children need a great deal of motor practice at each stage of development to develop the muscular control and memory that is needed for the stages that follow.

How Is Physical Development Facilitated?

Large muscles develop as children are given opportunities to engage in a wide range of movement activities. Teachers should provide the equipment, space, activities, and time for children to use their muscles and to develop the subtle shifts in balance needed for fluid movement.

Physical skills develop primarily through play but can also be encouraged through selected teacher-directed activities. Because children enjoy physical activities and readily engage in them, it is easy to overlook those children who shy away from particular types of motor activities because they lack the skill or confidence to try them. Be sure children have ample opportunities to develop the wide range of large and small muscle skills. Invite reluctant children into activities, playing with them as they begin to develop skills in a new area.

Large muscle skills include running and the use of slides, ladders, ramps, swings, balance beams, balls, sand and water table tools, tricycles, wagons, and a variety of outdoor surfaces.

Small muscle skills are developed through the use of a wide variety of materials such as manipulative toys, blocks, puzzles, books, art materials, writing materials, clay, and rhythm instruments.

The activities presented in this chapter help children strengthen both gross and fine motor skills and cultivate the eye-hand coordination that affects perceptual and cognitive development.

ARCHITECTS UNDER CONSTRUCTION

SKILL: PHYSICAL DEVELOPMENT—LARGE MUSCLES

OBJECTIVES:

1. To increase control and balance in building with unit blocks
2. To develop visual tracking skills
3. To develop spatial awareness and perceptual motor abilities
4. To practice distinguishing foreground from background objects
5. To develop eye-hand coordination

DESCRIPTION:

Take a photograph of a child's block structure. Transfer it to the computer and enlarge it to 5 × 7 inches. Print the photo. Label it with the child's name and description or name of the structure.

Punch ring holes in the copies and put the pages into a three-ring binder as part of a class-made book entitled *Architectural Digest*. Invite children to look at the book and choose a structure to build by using the photo as a blueprint.

EXTENSIONS:

Small-Group Activities:

Take photographs of familiar buildings in the community and enlarge each to 8 × 10 inches. Punch ring holes in the pages and put them into a three-ring binder. Invite a few children to choose a picture of a building to construct and work together to build.

An optional activity is to take a photograph of a child's block structure, print it, and add it to the book, putting it on the page opposite the picture of the real building.

Independent Explorations:

The child can draw a building and then construct it with unit blocks, using the drawing as a blueprint. Later, the teacher can take a photograph of the construction and ask the child to compare the photograph to the drawing, reflecting on his or her work.

One-on-One Instruction:

In the building area of the classroom, invite the child to use wooden unit blocks to plan and construct a building with a specific number of floors. Take a photograph of the

child and completed structure. Print it. Instruct the child to count and record the number of floors on the page. Add the page to the *Architectural Digest.*

Family Involvement:

Send home a 20-piece set of unit blocks, foam or wood. Include a note instructing the parents to build a structure with the blocks and to invite their child to copy it. Parents and child may take turns building the model and copying it.

LOOK AT WHAT I CAN DO

SKILL: PHYSICAL DEVELOPMENT—LARGE MUSCLE COORDINATION AND SPATIAL AWARENESS

OBJECTIVES:

1. To learn to focus attention
2. To develop balance
3. To develop an awareness of body/space relationships
4. To increase ability to reproduce specific movements accurately

DESCRIPTION:

Take individual photographs of children performing different body movements. Enlarge the photos to at least 5 × 7 inches and print them. Cut out the pictures, mount them on construction paper, and laminate them as cards.

Place the cards face down on the floor. Invite children to take turns being the leader, choosing a card and performing the movement shown. Then challenge the class to copy the leader's movement.

EXTENSIONS:

Small-Group Activities:

As an introduction to the activity, gather a small group of children. Invite a child to be the leader and to perform a body movement. Tell the leader to chant, "This is what I can do. Everybody do it too." Tell the others to copy the leader. Take a photograph of the leader performing the movement and use it later as a transition activity, proceeding as described above.

Independent Explorations:

Place the movement cards in an open area so that children can look at them and try the movements on their own.

One-on-One Instruction:

To make the activity more challenging for young readers, write the name of the movement on the back of the card and ask the child to read it. After the child attempts to read it, tell the child to turn the card over to see whether he or she was correct by looking at the photo. Then tell the child to perform the movement.

Family Involvement:

Send home a note asking parents to take turns performing and copying various body movements or exercises with their child.

Invite parents who know Yoga or Tai Chi positions or movements to come to class and teach them to the children. Take photographs of those parents and make a set of cards for later classroom use.

HOW DOES IT MOVE?

SKILL: PHYSICAL DEVELOPMENT—LARGE MUSCLE COORDINATION AND LOCOMOTOR SKILLS

OBJECTIVES:

1. To develop motor-planning skills
2. To use creative movement for self-expression
3. To increase motor development
4. To increase kinesthetic awareness
5. To develop motor memory

DESCRIPTION:

During a class excursion, take digital photographs of inanimate objects that can move. For example, at the fire station you might take photographs of a fire truck, a gurney, an extension ladder, a fire hose shooting water, or a rotating flashing light. At school, print out the photographs and enlarge them to 8 × 10 inches.

As a group activity, have the children take turns choosing and identifying the object in a photograph and moving like the object in operation. Challenge the children to recall the motion verbally.

EXTENSIONS:

Small-Group Activities:

To make a *Creative Movement Classroom Book,* take photographs of the children performing the movements of the objects. Print and put the pictures into page protectors. Place the original photo of the object into a page protector and secure it in a three-ring binder on the page opposite the photo of the children performing the motion.

Make an individual book for each excursion. Invite small groups of children to look at the book; discuss the objects and movements. Ask each child to choose a favorite movement and to form a group with other children who like that movement best. Place a line along the floor and have one child from each group stand on it. Tell the other members of each group to form a line behind their first member on the line, making a "human graph" of their favorite movements. Later, the children could record the outcome on a real graph.

Independent Explorations:

Take photographs of objects in the classroom or on the playground that suggest specific movements (e.g., scissors, stapler, swing, ball, umbrella). Enlarge, print, mount, and laminate the pictures. Place them in the movement center for children to select independently. Their job is to look at a picture and then pretend their bodies are that object and move as it would, repeating for each picture.

One-on-One Instruction:

Gather some objects from the classroom that suggest movement. Place them in a box. Instruct the child to choose one. Then ask the child to act out the movement of the object. Try to guess the object as the child performs, as in a game of charades.

Family Involvement:

Suggest that the children take turns borrowing the *Creative Movement Classroom Book.* Send home a note with the book, encouraging parents to try to perform the motions with their child or to suggest other ways to show the motions of the objects.

FOLLOW THE FLAG

SKILL: PHYSICAL DEVELOPMENT—BALANCE AND FIGURE/GROUND DISCRIMINATION

OBJECTIVES:

1. To increase spatial awareness
2. To increase awareness of directionality
3. To copy movements
4. To develop large muscle coordination

DESCRIPTION:

Take individual photographs of children in different positions and holding two different-colored flags. Flags can be made by taping short crepe paper strips to tongue depressors or by stapling them onto stiff cardboard strips.

Enlarge the photographs to 8×10 inches and print them. Mount and laminate the pictures or put them into page protectors. Secure the pages together with large book rings or in a three-ring binder. Choose one page to show to a small group of children. Give each child two flags, the same colors as in the photograph. Invite the children to copy the position, using the flags.

EXTENSIONS:

Small-Group Activities:

Obtain pictures of air traffic flag signals. Tell the group what the signal means and then invite one child to copy the position. Encourage other children to pretend to be airplanes obeying the flag signal. Invite children to take turns giving the signals and being the airplanes.

For more of a challenge, ask one child to choose a photograph and to give verbal directions about where to position the flags before actually performing the position for others to copy.

Independent Explorations:

Place in a box on the playground the colored flags and the photographs of children holding positions. During outside play, individual children may copy the positions, using the flags.

One-on-One Instruction:

Give only verbal directions for the child to follow. For example, say, "Hold the red flag in your right hand. Hold the blue flag in your left hand. Put your right hand above your head. Put your left hand straight in front of your body."

Family Involvement:

Send home two sets of blue and red flags made by the children. Include directions for the parents for taking turns with their child using the flags to create and copy positions.

DO THE LOCOMOTION

SKILL: PHYSICAL DEVELOPMENT—KINESTHETIC AWARENESS AND POSITION IN SPACE

OBJECTIVES:

1. To practice following directions
2. To increase motor skills
3. To participate in a group
4. To practice moving in a variety of ways
5. To develop an awareness of where the body is in space

DESCRIPTION:

Take photographs of five objects on the playground. Take photographs of children moving in five different ways, such as hopping, jumping, crawling, running, skipping, or walking backward. Enlarge the photos to at least 5 × 7 inches and print them. Mount the pictures on construction paper cards. Color-code the cards by making red dots on the backs of the object cards and black dots on the backs of the method cards. Laminate if desired.

Divide the cards into two groups: (a) the object cards (which show the destination) and (b) the method cards (which show the type of locomotion). Invite one child to choose an object card and name the destination pictured there. Invite another child to choose a method card and name the type of locomotion pictured.

Have all the children move toward the object, using the method of locomotion indicated. When all the children arrive at the destination, tell two other children to choose additional cards and to proceed in the same manner. Continue until all the children have had a chance to choose a card or until interest declines.

EXTENSIONS:

Small-Group Activities:

Conduct a relay race. Pick an object card. Make a starting line 15 feet away from the object indicated. Tell the children to form two relay lines behind the starting point. Pick a method card to determine how the children will move to the object. Show the children the card and have them participate in a relay race, moving as indicated to the object and returning to tap the next person in line. The first group to finish chooses the next object and method.

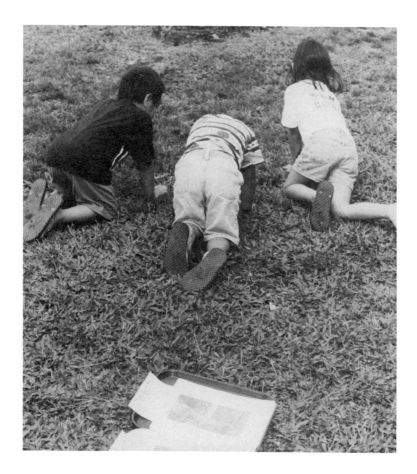

Independent Explorations:

On the playground, mark off a track that is 4 feet wide and 15 feet long. Place method of locomotion cards in a basket at the starting line. The child can choose a card and move to the finish line in the method indicated.

One-on-One Instruction:

Instruct the child to choose a locomotion card and to perform the movement in place, without moving forward. Encourage the child to try the movement again, this time moving backward.

Family Involvement:

Send home a duplicate copy of the method cards and a blank set of cards. Instruct family members to help the child draw on the blank cards objects found outdoors near their home. Include directions for playing locomotion games with family members.

TACTILE MATS

SKILL: PHYSICAL DEVELOPMENT—EYE-HAND COORDINATION

OBJECTIVES:

1. To practice spatial estimation
2. To increase small muscle control
3. To learn figure/ground discrimination

DESCRIPTION:

Take a photograph of a familiar object and enlarge it to at least 4 inches square. Print and laminate it or place it in a page protector. Place the picture on a table and invite children to replicate the object's shape by using three-dimensional material such as modeling clay or biodegradable packing material.

Show the children how to form small rolls or snakes from modeling clay and to press the pieces together to form an outline of the object. Some children may choose to fill in the whole shape itself. When using biodegradable packing material, show the children how to press one piece on a damp sponge and stick the pieces together to copy the shape.

EXTENSIONS:

Small-Group Activities:

Invite children to use modeling clay to make shapes or objects. Take digital photographs of the children's designs. Enlarge, print, and laminate the photos as described above and label them with the designers' names. Place them in a box in the sensory center. Encourage children to copy their classmates' designs.

Independent Explorations:

Place a wet sponge and a container of biodegradable packing material on a table in the art area for making abstract, three-dimensional structures.

One-on-One Instruction:

Invite the child to use modeling clay to copy numbers or alphabet letters on laminated sheets. The child may place the modeling clay directly on the printed letter or number or form it adjacent to the pattern.

Family Involvement:

Send home a 2-foot length of string or yarn in a plastic bag. Include a note asking parents to help their child form one shape or letter with the string. The next day in school, ask the child to recall and reproduce the shape made at home. Take a photograph of the string shape, print and laminate it, and use it as a pattern for classmates to use with modeling clay.

SORTING OUT THE THEMES

SKILL: PHYSICAL DEVELOPMENT—SMALL MUSCLE CONTROL AND EYE-HAND COORDINATION

OBJECTIVES:

1. To increase sorting skills and classification skills
2. To improve fine motor skills
3. To develop eye-hand coordination
4. To improve memory skills

DESCRIPTION:

Take photographs of children throughout the year participating in activities that involve a particular theme. Photos may be taken on excursions or in school. Print two sets of 3×5-inch photos. Keep one set to make a classroom memory book of the theme and projects as described below. Make the other set available for children to use in class.

Ask the children to cut out the pictures, spread paste on the backs, and mount them on 4×6-inch cards. After the paste is dry, laminate the cards. After picture cards have been made for at least two themes, invite the children to sort the pictures by thematic categories. Children may work individually or in small groups.

EXTENSIONS:

Small-Group Activities:

Provide a small group of children with picture cards from a specific theme. Ask them to take turns pointing to and dictating what's happening in the picture. Record each response under the photograph and ask the child to sign his or her name. On a separate card, write the name of the theme and record what the children liked about the theme. Use this card as the title page. Bind together with the photograph cards to make a memory book.

Independent Explorations:

Display a theme-based memory book. Place magazines, scissors, paste, and construction paper on the table. Children can find magazine pictures that relate to or remind them of the theme. They can make a collage by cutting out the pictures and pasting them onto construction paper.

One-on-One Instruction:

Place 4 to 10 photograph cards from a recent project into a basket on a table. Invite the child to look at the cards and describe what's happening in the photograph. Ask the child to line up the cards in order of occurrence.

For a greater challenge, use number cards and invite the child to place the picture cards under the number in order of occurrence.

Family Involvement:

Send home a sheet of construction paper along with a note requesting photographs from a family trip, celebration, or other event. Ask parents to let their child choose some photographs from a favorite activity and paste them onto the construction paper. Ask that the completed project be returned to school for sharing with classmates during group time.

LACE A FAVORITE

SKILL: PHYSICAL DEVELOPMENT—SMALL MUSCLE CONTROL AND EYE-HAND COORDINATION

OBJECTIVES:

1. To increase spatial awareness
2. To increase directionality awareness
3. To practice decision making
4. To improve finger strength and dexterity

DESCRIPTION:

Take photographs of children engaged in activities during the course of a day. Size the photographs to fit into the middle of a paper plate and then print the photos. Ask each of the children to choose a photograph of a favorite activity, whether they are in the picture or not.

After a child chooses a picture, direct her to glue the photograph onto a paper plate. Show the child how to punch holes around the edge of the plate, assisting as necessary. Give the child a 2-foot length of yarn, with masking tape secured around one end to make the tip stiff enough to use as a sewing needle. Instruct the child to sew around the plate by pulling the yarn either under and over, or up and down. Write or have the child write her name on the back of the paper plate and dictate what she liked about the activity captured in the photograph.

EXTENSIONS:

Small-Group Activities:

Take photographs from a recent excursion or project and print them. Trim the paper around each printed photo to an 8½-inch square. Punch holes evenly around the edges of each photo square. Invite each child to choose a photograph. Have the children take turns lacing their photo squares to others until a "quilt" is completed. Display the quilt in the classroom to commemorate a special event.

Independent Explorations:

Arrange photographs, scissors, paper plates, glue, and a hole punch on a table. Children can make Favorite Photo Plates for their classmates to lace.

One-on-One Instruction:

After the child has chosen a favorite picture, glue it to a rectangular piece of poster board. Punch two rows of parallel holes around the edges and give the child instructions for sewing a series of small X shapes around the picture to form a border.

Family Involvement:

Send home the child's laced picture. Instruct parents to ask their child to talk about the picture and to record the child's words on the back of the paper plate. Request that they return it to school with their child for sharing at group time.

PHOTO PLACE MATS

SKILL: PHYSICAL DEVELOPMENT—SMALL MUSCLE
CONTROL AND EYE-HAND COORDINATION

OBJECTIVES:

1. To practice opposing motions by using scissors to cut
2. To improve tactile awareness
3. To improve motor accuracy using a pencil
4. To develop finger strength

DESCRIPTION:

Say that the group will make personalized place mats for lunch or snack time. Ask the children to choose an object, scene, or themselves to photograph. Take a digital photograph of each child's choice. Enlarge the photos to 5 × 7 inches and print them.

Direct each child to spread glue or paste carefully on the back of the photo and then to turn the paper over and press it into the middle of a 9 × 12-inch sheet of construction paper to form a place mat. Direct the children to write their names on their construction paper place mats above their photos. Laminate the place mats and use them during lunch or snack time.

EXTENSIONS:

Small-Group Activities:

Invite two or three children to cut pictures out of magazines and to glue them onto a 9 × 12-inch sheet of construction paper. Instruct them to sign their names by the pictures they have chosen. Laminate or cover with clear contact paper to make a mat for use with modeling clay or during snack time.

Independent Explorations:

Place glue, scissors, markers, and paper on a table in the art area with a stack of photographs and magazine pictures for exploration.

One-on-One Instruction:

For more practice with fine motor skills, invite the child to use alphabet stencils with fine markers to form the letters of his or her name on a place mat.

Family Involvement:

Send home a sheet of construction paper and an 18-inch length of clear contact paper. Encourage parents to look through magazines or family photographs with their child to find pictures to make a special family place mat.

SILHOUETTES

SKILL: PHYSICAL DEVELOPMENT—SMALL MUSCLE CONTROL AND VISUAL TRACKING

OBJECTIVES:

1. To increase spatial awareness
2. To improve visual matching skills
3. To develop figure/ground discrimination
4. To refine eye movements

DESCRIPTION:

Photograph an object. Transfer the photo to the computer and print it. Create a silhouette or outline of the same object by using the editing feature; print it.

Continue in the same manner for the number of desired objects until you have two sets of pictures for each object—silhouettes and colored prints.

During group time, hand out the silhouette pictures. Invite children to name the object that is silhouetted. Line up the photographs and ask one child at a time to match his or her silhouette to its corresponding picture.

EXTENSIONS:

Small-Group Activities:

After creating eight different silhouettes from the photographs on the computer, use the layout program to make game boards with two rows of four silhouettes each. Position the silhouettes differently for each game board. Print out the four game boards. Laminate if desired. Invite children to play a lotto game: Show them a color photograph; instruct them find the corresponding silhouette and to place a marker over it. Continue until all silhouettes are covered.

Independent Explorations:

Place a set of pictures and silhouettes on a table and invite children to match the color photographs with the silhouettes.

One-on-One Instruction:

Show the child a silhouette and ask him or her to locate the real object in the classroom.

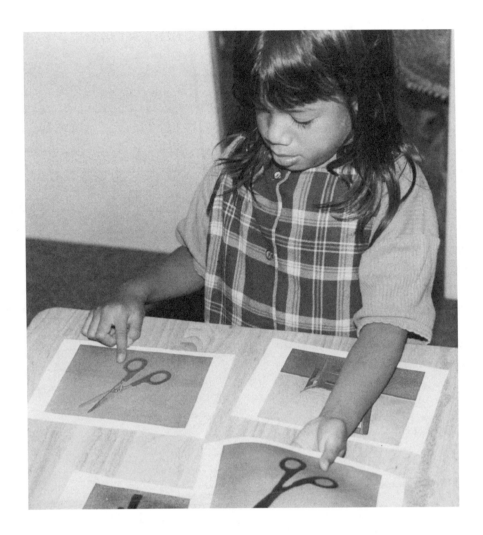

Family Involvement:

Write a note home, encouraging parents to trace around kitchen utensils or common household tools on a large sheet of paper to create silhouettes and then to invite their child to match each real item with its silhouette, name the item, and discuss its use.

PHYSICAL DEVELOPMENT CHECKLIST

	Baseline	Period 1	Period 2
Child: _____	__/__/__	__/__/__	__/__/__

	Baseline	Period 1	Period 2
To improve muscle strength			
To improve balance			
To improve motor control			
To develop motor-planning skills			
To develop perceptual motor skills			
To develop kinesthetic awareness			
To improve motor memory			
To increase coordination			
To reproduce movements			
To reproduce movement patterns			
To express oneself through creative movement			
To increase awareness of position in space			
To increase awareness of directionality			
To improve eye-hand coordination			
To develop figure/ground discrimination			

To develop large muscle skills:

	Baseline	Period 1	Period 2
Walking			
Running			
Hopping			
Skipping			
Jumping			
Throwing			

To develop small muscle skills:

	Baseline	Period 1	Period 2
Writing			
Tearing			
Cutting			
Pouring			
Coloring			
Painting			
Gluing			

CODE: ✔ = Does Consistently   ± = Does Sometimes   × = Does Rarely/Does Not Do

6

MATHEMATICS

MATHEMATICS INTRODUCTION

What Is Mathematics?

Mathematics is a way of thinking that enables children to begin to organize and understand their world. It is more than just numbers and counting and rules. It arises from an attempt to solve problems with space, shapes, time, size, patterns, quantities, and relationships.

Why Is Mathematics Important?

If mathematics is one way for children to make sense of their world, then mathematical thinking is more crucial now than ever. Children of the 21st century live in an information age dominated by the technology of computers, calculators, digitized data, and complicated machines. The computer affords access to a world of information that needs to be gathered, organized, analyzed, interpreted, and disseminated. Mathematics and mathematical thinking are indispensable in the modern society.

How Is Mathematics Learned?

Mathematics learning is a lengthy process that begins in infancy and continues to develop through childhood. It evolves through direct experience with real objects in play and daily life. Mathematics is learned through the rhythms of a mother's heartbeat and as infants develop patterns of eating and sleeping. They notice patterns as they begin to recognize the faces of Mom and Dad. Babies lay the foundation for spatial awareness by becoming aware of their bodies as they explore with their hands and feet. Through exploration and games like Peekaboo, toddlers discover object constancy, a necessary concept for developing thinking and number skills. A young child starts to understand one-to-one correspondence as she counts the three candles on her birthday cake or holds up three fingers, giving each one a number.

Later, children explore shapes and colors and notice similarities and differences. While setting a table or putting away toys on a shelf, they are learning sorting and counting skills. The preschooler who completes puzzles demonstrates spatial awareness, and when he anticipates lunch, he demonstrates an awareness of time.

How Is Mathematical Thinking Facilitated?

Adults must provide opportunities for children to develop the mathematical reasoning necessary to live in today's complex, fast-paced society. Because young children learn best through hands-on experiences, mathematical concepts should be embedded in daily play and routines. Simple tasks such as using measuring cups and spoons in sand and water play, matching shoes, and putting one sock on each foot make mathematics meaningful for children. Facilitate and extend mathematical literacy by modeling the language of mathematics and by helping children name and describe their thinking and discoveries.

Provide a math-rich environment filled with opportunities to investigate relationships between materials and develop activities targeted to explore areas of mathematical learning that include the following:

- Matching
- Sorting and classifying
- Patterning
- Counting and comparing
- Exploring shapes
- Estimating
- Measuring
- One-to-one correspondence
- Geometry
- Time

- Spatial relationships
- Seriation
- Number concepts like more and less

A PLACE FOR EVERYTHING

SKILL: MATHEMATICS—SORTING

Note: This activity is particularly effective at the beginning of the school year.

OBJECTIVES:

1. To group objects according to where they are used
2. To identify and organize familiar objects
3. To improve problem-solving skills

DESCRIPTION:

Invite each child to choose an object in the classroom. Take a digital photograph of each object. Print, mount, and laminate the pictures. Place them in a gift bag. Also take a digital photograph of each learning center in the classroom. Enlarge these photographs to 8 × 10-inch prints. Mount and laminate each one.

During group time, invite each child to pick a picture from the bag, name the object, describe its use, and place it under the learning center picture where it belongs. If the child has difficulty, ask the child who originally chose the object to help.

EXTENSIONS:

Small-Group Activities:

Invite children to take turns choosing a picture, naming it, and finding the real object in the classroom.

Independent Explorations:

Mount clear pockets under the pictures of the learning centers. Place a set of object cards in a basket for independent sorting into learning centers.

One-on-One Instruction:

After the child has sorted the object pictures by learning centers, ask her or him to group by a different attribute. Say, "Think of another way to sort the pictures." If the child has difficulty, suggest sorting by color, material (e.g., wood, plastic, fabric) or similar use (e.g., writing/drawing implement, reading material, building).

Family Involvement:

Take photographs of children playing in the different learning centers. Print, label, mount, and laminate the pictures. Make copies of the pictures of the objects children chose and send home a sorting game with directions for use.

LOOK AT MY DAY

SKILL: MATHEMATICS—SEQUENCING/TIME

OBJECTIVES:

1. To gain a beginning understanding of time
2. To understand the concepts of before and after
3. To recall a sequence of events
4. To use ordinal numbers

DESCRIPTION:

Take digital photographs of children engaged in activities during the school day. Print the photos, mount them on 4 × 6-inch colored paper, and laminate them.

Gather the children and share the pictures with the group. Invite the children to choose a picture. Ask what happens first in the school day, what comes after, and so on. Using the pictures, discuss with the group the concepts of before and after.

Then have the children come up to the front with their pictures and stand left to right, in the order the action in their pictures occurs. After they agree on the sequence, mount the pictures on cardboard. Place a clothespin as a marker next to the picture of the first event of the day and move it as children progress from one activity to another.

EXTENSIONS:

Small-Group Activities:

Display the chart depicting the daily sequence of events, as described above. Glue a picture of a clock showing the time for each activity or transition next to the photograph of it on the chart. Make copies of the clock and activity pictures. Invite children to select a clock picture, tell the time, and match it with the clock on the chart. Have them look through the activity cards and find an activity that happens at that time.

Independent Explorations:

Place a set of activity cards in a box on a table adjacent to a pocket chart that has been mounted on the wall. Invite children to sequence the activity cards by placing them in order of occurrence from top to bottom.

One-on-One Instruction:

Make a five-pocket chart labeled with the ordinal numbers 1st, 2nd, 3rd, 4th, and 5th. Point out the ordinal numbers to the child. Ask the child to look at the set of activity cards, to pick the activity that comes first in the day, and to put it in the corresponding pocket. Have the child continue placing the cards in order of occurrence from left to right and identifying each ordinal number in the sequence.

Family Involvement:

Take photographs of other activities that are sequenced, such as hand washing, toileting, nap/rest preparation, and lunch procedures. Make sequencing game folders for children to take home and share with parents.

THE SHAPE OF THINGS

SKILL: MATHEMATICS—SPATIAL RELATIONSHIPS/GEOMETRY

OBJECTIVES:

1. To identify and recognize shapes
2. To make shapes
3. To count the number of sides in a shape
4. To match three-dimensional shapes with their two-dimensional photographs

DESCRIPTION:

Show the children a paper triangle. Have them count the number of sides. Then provide them with rope or sticks to make triangle shapes of their own. Have the children try to move their bodies to make the shape with their friends (show how to place three sticks to form a triangle and then invite three children to form a triangle with their bodies). Use this procedure with a variety of shapes.

Take photographs of the children forming the shapes. Print, mount, and laminate the photos. Instruct the children to match each photograph with the corresponding cutout shape. Invite children to find shapes around the room and to match each with the photograph of the children forming the shape.

EXTENSIONS:

Small-Group Activities:

Draw basic shapes on large cards. After the children locate objects in the room that represent these basic shapes, take photographs of them and make a sorting game. Place the picture cards face down and invite children to take turns choosing a card and placing it on the matching shape.

Independent Explorations:

Place craft sticks and a 12-inch length of rope on a tray. Place in a box the photographs of children forming various shapes. Leave these on a table in the math area. Children can use the craft sticks or rope to form the shapes in the photographs.

One-on-One Instruction:

Place at least 16 craft sticks on a tray. Ask the child to form a square with some of the sticks. If the child has difficulty, make a square with four sticks, count the four sides,

and note that each side is the same length. After the child is able to form a square with four sticks, say, "Now make a bigger square, using more sticks." Ask the child to make other shapes, increasing the challenge according to individual ability and interest.

Family Involvement:

Send home a note asking parents to help their child find and identify shape objects at home and to let their child bring one object to school for sharing. Take photographs of the home objects and add them to the existing game.

EATING BY NUMBERS

SKILL: MATHEMATICS—ONE-TO-ONE CORRESPONDENCE/MATCHING

OBJECTIVES:

1. To gain an interest in counting
2. To gain an understanding of one-to-one correspondence
3. To match shapes

DESCRIPTION:

Over the course of several days, take a photograph of each snack available for the day. Crop the individual food items and enlarge them to actual size. Print the photos. Put the photos into page protectors. Place the real food items in containers on the snack table.

Remind children to wash their hands and then invite them to match the real food items to the pictured items by putting the food on top of the picture. After children have matched all the food items, they may eat the snacks and enjoy. To add interest, use food cut into different shapes to make an object corresponding to a current theme. For example, for a unit on fire safety, children can make "burnt matches" by putting pitted black olives on the tops of thin carrot sticks.

EXTENSIONS:

Small-Group Activities:

Invite children to make a pattern with different-shaped food items. For example, a pattern might be one cheese slice, two apple slices. Take a photograph of the food pattern and display it for other children to copy before eating.

Independent Explorations:

Provide a variety of different-shaped crackers for children to graph on laminated grids before eating them.

One-on-One Instruction:

Place a variety of different-shaped cereals on a tray. Ask the child to count out a specific amount and shape to eat. (Note: Always check for food allergies before presenting any food activity.)

Family Involvement:

Send home snack pictures with suggestions for parents to talk about numbers and shapes with their child as they eat.

CALL ME

SKILL: MATHEMATICS—NUMBER MATCHING/NUMERAL RECOGNITION

OBJECTIVES:

1. To identify numerals
2. To match numerals
3. To replicate a sequence of numerals

DESCRIPTION:

Make a class telephone book. Take a photograph of each child and teacher. Crop each photograph to a head shot measuring 3 inches square. Type the child's or teacher's name and telephone number under the photograph. Print out a page for each child and teacher. Take photographs of real or toy emergency vehicles. Type the emergency telephone number or 911 under each vehicle and print out on one page. Include this as the first page of the telephone book.

Take a photograph of the classroom telephone and mount it on construction paper to create a cover for the telephone book. Arrange the photo pages in alphabetical order by person's name and bind the pages into a classroom telephone book.

Invite the children to find their pages in the telephone book and to use a play telephone to dial their telephone numbers.

EXTENSIONS:

Small-Group Activities:

After receiving permission from parents, invite children to copy classmates' names and telephone numbers and to make individual telephone books to take home.

Independent Explorations:

Make copies of the classroom telephone book for each child to use in dramatic play, as they pretend to call each other.

One-on-One Instruction:

Give the child a telephone number and ask her to find the person it belongs to by looking in the telephone book. After she finds the correct telephone number, ask her to identify the numerals and to dial them on a play telephone.

Family Involvement:

Send home the individual telephone books and ask parents to help their child identify classmates' names and telephone numbers.

COUNTING ON YOU

SKILL: MATHEMATICS—MEANINGFUL COUNTING/NUMERAL RECOGNITION

OBJECTIVES:

1. To engage in meaningful counting
2. To learn one-to-one correspondence
3. To improve number recognition skills

DESCRIPTION:

Take individual photographs of children in costumes, engaged in dramatic play. Print and mount the pictures on lightweight cardboard. Cut around each body shape. Glue a felt or magnetic strip onto the back of each picture.

As the children watch, choose a felt or magnetic numeral. Place the correct number of child photographs under the numeral, using a flannel or magnetic board as appropriate.

EXTENSIONS:

Small-Group Activities:

Pass around a basket of felt numerals and invite each child to choose one. The children can take turns identifying the numerals and placing the correct number of photographs below the numeral on the flannel board.

Independent Explorations:

Have children make number sets using pictures and erasable markers. In a basket next to a stack of vinyl place mats, place photographs of the children. Invite children to make number sets by putting photographs on a place mat, counting them, and using a marker to write the numeral on the place mat.

One-on-One Instruction:

Play a sorting game with the photographs by instructing the child to sort them by gender, hair color, or eye color. Determine which group has more or less by counting and comparing the number of children in each group.

Family Involvement:

Print digitized photographs of individual children and send a set home with each child. Direct parents to help their child cut out some of the pictures and then glue one or more pictures to sheets of paper. Then the child should write the numeral of the number of pictures glued onto each sheet. To make a number book, child and parents could staple the sheets together in numerical order.

TREASURE HUNT

SKILL: MATHEMATICS—MATCHING

OBJECTIVES:

1. To improve matching skills
2. To improve visual perception skills
3. To follow directions

DESCRIPTION:

Take photographs of items in the classroom and outside on the playground. Print them, cut out the individual items, and mount them on tagboard to make clue cards. Laminate or cover them with contact paper.

Make several treasure hunt sets, each containing three photo clue cards (either all indoor objects or all outdoor objects) and an index card divided into three sections. Number the index card sections 1, 2, and 3. Write one of those numbers on the back of each of the clue cards. Put each set of cards into an envelope. Invite a child to choose one of the envelopes and to locate each object pictured. At each pictured object will be a self-inking stamp (that you placed there beforehand). Tell the child to stamp the index card in the space that corresponds to the number. After all the clues have been located and the index card has been completely stamped, have the child return it to you for a treasure (e.g., sticker, stamp, other small reward).

As another activity, give an inside photo clue card to each child. Ask each child in turn to find the object pictured on her or his card. After the group has practiced a few times, give each child an outside photo clue card. Then try the treasure hunt game outdoors.

EXTENSIONS:

Small-Group Activities:

Conduct the treasure hunt as a small-group activity inside the classroom. To make the treasure hunt more difficult, use five picture card clues before the treasure can be found.

Independent Explorations:

Make several treasure hunt sets containing three picture clue cards each. Label each clue card on the back with a number to indicate the order of the hunt. Put each set

in an envelope. Children can choose an envelope and follow the numbered clues to find the treasure.

One-on-One Instruction:

Ask the child to draw a picture to be used as a treasure. Instruct the child to choose three inside photo cards as clues and to make a treasure hunt game. Talk about what the first, second, and third clue will be and where to place the treasure. Suggest that the child invite a friend to play the game.

Family Involvement:

Send home directions for playing the treasure hunt at home. Suggest that parents draw pictures or write words about where to find the next clue and read them to their child.

For an additional parent involvement activity, make a video of the children playing the game at school (always obtain parental permission before videotaping the children) and show it at a parent meeting. Talk about the language, mathematics, and social skills the children are learning while playing this game.

EXERCISE BY THE DAY

SKILL: MATHEMATICS—COUNTING AND CONCEPT OF TIME

OBJECTIVES:

1. To participate in counting through meaningful experience
2. To improve number recognition skills
3. To become acquainted with the calendar and the concept of time
4. To develop large motor skills

DESCRIPTION:

Take individual photographs of children doing a specific exercise. Resize each photo to a 3½-inch square. Print and cut out the pictures. Mount six exercise photos on a 4-inch cube. (The cube can be made from two half-gallon milk cartons cut to 4 inches high. Stuff one cut-down carton with crumpled newspaper and push the other carton into it. Cover the cube with wood-grained contact paper and glue or tape a photo to each side.)

Invite children to take turns identifying the day of the month and then rolling the exercise block. The exercise photo that lands on top is the exercise of the day. Direct students to do as many of that exercise as the number of the day. For example, if the cube lands on the hopping exercise and it is May 6, the children hop 6 times.

EXTENSIONS:

Small-Group Activities:

Make a large Styrofoam die. Instruct one child to roll the die and to count the number of dots on the top side. Instruct another child to roll the exercise cube. Have all the children do the rolled number of the rolled exercise.

Independent Explorations:

Put exercise cubes in a basket outside on the playground. Label the basket with a large numeral. Individual children may roll the block and perform the exercise the number of times indicated by the numeral.

One-on-One Instruction:

Instruct the child to roll the exercise cube and to identify the exercise. Next, ask the child to roll a die and to count the number of dots on top. Finally, ask the child to perform the indicated number of exercises.

Family Involvement:

Send home an exercise block and number card set along with instructions. Invite family members to play the exercise game with the child.

PART OF THE WHOLE

SKILL: MATHEMATICS—PART TO WHOLE

OBJECTIVES:

1. To improve spatial awareness in a meaningful context
2. To develop an understanding of part to whole
3. To improve problem-solving skills
4. To develop visual discrimination skills

DESCRIPTION:

Take photographs of objects or people familiar to the children. Enlarge each of the pictures to 8 × 10 inches and print them. Remove a segment from each picture. Print a series of the pictures with an additional segment removed from each subsequent photograph.

Show a child the photo with the fewest pieces of identifying information first and ask him to guess what it is. If he is unable to do so, show the next in the series of pictures until the child is able to identify the subject.

EXTENSIONS:

Small-Group Activities:

Print out an additional set of complete photographs of the children in the class. Cut a rectangle approximately 1 × ½ inch from the middle of a sheet of black construction paper. Cover the photograph with the paper, positioning the cutout to reveal only the eyes of the child in the photograph. Invite children to guess the identity of the classmate. Move the rectangular window around to reveal different features until someone guesses correctly.

Independent Explorations:

Cover a picture with a window template. Have the child open a window and try to guess what the picture is. Proceed with opening windows to revel portions of the picture until the child can identify it.

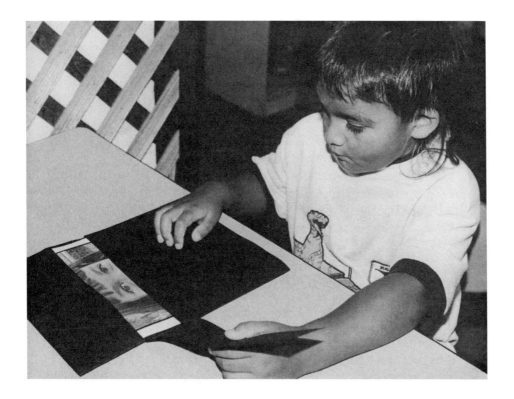

One-on-One Instruction:

Before the child opens a template window, ask, "What window would you like to open? What part would you like to see?" Encourage the child to name the position of the window instead of just pointing to it. Give help when necessary.

Family Involvement:

Make copies of each series of pictures and put them into file folders. Attach directions for playing the game. Urge parents to work with their child, taking turns identifying the picture.

Ask parents to send a photograph to class with their child. Scan the photo and reproduce as described above for use in small groups.

BIG, BIGGER, BIGGEST

SKILL: MATHEMATICS—SERIATION

OBJECTIVES:

1. To practice comparison skills
2. To explore the concept of size
3. To develop skills in seriation
4. To improve visual discrimination

DESCRIPTION:

Take a photograph of a familiar object. Print it. Reduce the size of the photograph by 50% and print it. Enlarge the original photograph by 50% and print it. Cover each picture with clear contact paper or laminate it.

Give a child the three pictures and ask her to put them in order. If she is unsure of what to do, ask her to arrange them from smallest to largest or vice versa. For a greater challenge, make more sizes to seriate.

EXTENSIONS:

Small-Group Activities:

Adjust the brightness or shade of color instead of the size of the photograph for a different type of seriation game for children to play together. Place the set of photographs on the table with a pocket chart to use for a seriation activity.

Independent Explorations:

For variety, invite the children to seriate in different ways: left to right, top to bottom, biggest to smallest, smallest to biggest. Children can seriate the photographs and then explain the rationale.

Family Involvement:

Send home a note asking parents to find things at home to seriate with their child. Suggest ordering objects like measuring cups and spoons, shoes, dishes, and grades of sandpaper.

MATHEMATICS CHECKLIST

	Baseline	Period 1	Period 2
Child: _____	__/__/__	__/__/__	__/__/__

Spatial Relations and Geometry

To associate a part to its whole

To solve visual problems

To become aware of spatial relations

To match shapes

To form shapes

To count the sides of shapes

To match three-dimensional shapes with
their two-dimensional pictures

Numbers and Numerals

To count by rote

To count 1 to 10 objects

To experiment with the concept of numbers

To identify numerals

To match numbers to numerals

To use ordinal numbers

Categorization

To match objects

To match one-to-one

To sort objects by one attribute

To sort objects by two or more attributes

Sequence

To copy a sequence

To recall a sequence

Seriation

To compare objects by features

To seriate objects by features

Child: _____

Time

To experiment with the calendar

To sequence objects and events

To associate clocks with telling time

To locate events in time (before/after)

CODE:

✔ = Does Consistently

± = Does Sometimes

✕ = Does Rarely/Does Not Do

7

SENSORY
EXPLORATION

SENSORY EXPLORATION INTRODUCTION

What Is Sensory Exploration?

Sensory exploration is the examination of people and objects in the environment through one or more of the senses. It exposes children to a range of sights, sounds, tastes, smells, and textures.

Why Is Sensory Exploration Important?

Human beings have only a few ways of getting information from the outside world into their brains for processing and storage: through the five senses and through movement. Sensory learning is a primary method of absorbing information and of learning for infants and toddlers. Language is later added to sensory experiences to help young children think and talk about the world in which they live. Preschoolers and early elementary students still rely heavily on sensory learning.

Young children need a great deal of sensory experience before they are able to identify, discriminate, understand, remember, and label sensory experiences. The informa-

151

tion gained from this type of learning forms the basis of young children's rapidly developing cognitive world. Sensory learning literally helps children make sense out of their world.

How Is Sensory Input Processed?

The human body is one large sensory processor. It is designed to take in information from the eyes, ears, nose, mouth, and skin. Our skin is the largest organ of the human body. Awareness of touch is probably the first sense the newborn experiences. The tactile sense is a primary mode of learning for the young child, providing information on size, shape, texture, and temperature.

Smell is a primitive sense. In fact, the part of the brain that processes olfactory information is sometimes referred to as "the old nose brain." Animals, including humans, are warned about impending danger, sources of food, and even potential mates through their sense of smell.

Taste is one of our most enjoyable senses. Taste buds evaluate a material's degree of sweetness, sourness, saltiness, or bitterness. These four basic taste characteristics combine to provide an almost limitless array of gustatory experiences.

Hearing begins before birth, but learning to listen is a developed skill that requires a great deal of experience. Because there is no equivalent of an eyelid over the ear, young children must learn how to listen selectively. Deciding to exclude irrelevant or less significant sounds is as important as learning to pay attention to important auditory input. The auditory sense is critical to language acquisition and later to reading development.

One of the newborn's first acts is to open his eyes, but it will take quite a long time for him to make sense out of the confusion of lines, angles, and colors that come flooding in. Over time, the child's visual acuity will develop, as will his ability to discriminate objects and to understand and recall them.

How Is Sensory Exploration Facilitated?

Because sensory learning is so important, it should be at the heart of the early childhood curriculum. Look for ways to add sensory experiences to all learning activities.

Children are bombarded with sensory input from birth, but they may need help to isolate, explore, and understand these sensations. Think of the length of time a toddler can spend opening and closing a hand around modeling clay that has had sand added to alter the texture. Children benefit from having sensory experiences isolated and emphasized as they are described in words.

Fill children's environment with interesting sights, sounds, tastes, smells, and things to touch. Some school programs have learning centers devoted to sensory explorations. Other schools highlight sensory experiences through other parts of their programs. In either approach, isolate and focus on individual senses and model the vocabulary with which to discuss them. Plan ways to stimulate each of the children's senses throughout the day.

WHAT'S MISSING?

SKILL: SENSORY EXPLORATION—VISUAL PERCEPTION

OBJECTIVES:

1. To look at a picture with a missing part, visualize the whole, and identify the person or object pictured
2. To identify the missing part of the photograph
3. To draw the missing part

DESCRIPTION:

Take close-up photographs of various stuffed animals and dolls in the center. Place each digitized picture into a page layout program, frame it with a large box, and print it.

Next, select either the circle or the square from the tool palette. Place the cursor over one part of the picture, adjusting the size so that it covers one body part; for example, cover a teddy bear's eye. Fill the shape with the paper color so that when it is printed, this part of the picture will be omitted. Print the picture, which, for the teddy bear example, will reveal the photograph of the teddy bear missing an eye. Move the shape to cover another body part and print another picture. Repeat to make four or five pictures blocking out different body parts of the teddy bear. Laminate each picture or place each into a plastic page protector. Repeat the process for each of the stuffed animals and dolls photographed.

Show the group a whole picture and ask them to name the object pictured. Then display one of that object's altered pictures. Ask what body part is missing. Once the missing body part is named, point to the blocked portion of the picture and reaffirm the name of that body part. Repeat with the other pictures.

Let the group know that these pictures will be available in one of the centers. Their job is to figure out what body part is missing and then to use a grease pencil or dry marker to draw it on the page.

EXTENSIONS:

Small-Group Activities:

Choose four to six pairs of whole and altered photographs. Place the intact pictures face down in a row on the floor. Make a second row composed of altered pictures. Show the children how to play the game Concentration by selecting one card from the top row and one from the bottom. If the pictures match, the child keeps the cards. If not, the cards are replaced and another child may take a turn. The goal is for the children to remember where pictures are placed once they have been seen so that the children will

be able to make a match at their next turn. The game is over when all the pairs have been located.

Independent Explorations:

Place in a basket all the cards with one or more body parts covered and a photograph of one toy. Children can add the missing pieces. When they are finished, the children should erase their grease pencil markings with a small cloth and return the materials to the shelf for others to use.

One-on-One Instruction:

Receptive Language: Show the child the intact picture of a stuffed animal or doll and ask the child to name it. Then show one of the cards with a missing piece. Say, "Look. Something is missing from the picture." Point to what is missing and say, "Yes, the doll's eye is not there."

Expressive Language: Show the child the picture of a whole animal and ask the child to name it. Then show one of the cards with a missing piece. Say, "What is missing in this picture?" Have the child name the missing part. If the child is unable to identify it, name it and ask the child to repeat it.

Family Involvement:

Send home an envelope with one set of pictures, including the intact photograph and all the altered pictures. Include a grease pencil, a small wiping cloth, and directions on how parents and child can use this game together.

FUNNY FRIENDS

SKILL: SENSORY EXPLORATION—VISUAL CLOSURE

OBJECTIVES:

1. To scan a stack of partial pictures to form whole pictures
2. To look for visual cues

DESCRIPTION:

Have each child in turn stand in the same spot to have a full body photograph taken. The goal is to take a photo of approximately the same height and body proportions for each child. Mount the pictures on construction paper and laminate each one. Add a laminated title page—*Funny Friends*—of construction paper. Bind the pictures together along the left side with a spiral binding. Then cut each photograph horizontally into thirds, cutting along the same spot on each page. Each third of a page may then be turned independently, creating odd combinations of pictures.

Show the children the book and have them flip through the partial pages to re-create either funny figures or the whole pictures.

EXTENSIONS:

Small-Group Activities:

Tell each child in a group of five to eight to dress up in a different costume from the dramatic play area. Then photograph each child so that the pictured children appear approximately the same size. Laminate, spiral bind, and cut the pictures horizontally into thirds and then show the group their funny dress-up photographs.

Independent Explorations:

Print two additional sets of photographs. Include in each set one intact photograph and one photograph cut into strips for four different children. Place each set of materials into an envelope. The children can take out the strips from one of the sets and look for clues as to the identity of the pictured child. They can use the strips as puzzle pieces to construct the whole image of the child and then use the intact photographs to self-correct.

One-on-One Instruction:

Receptive Language: Use the *Funny Friends* book with the child. Flip randomly through the strips. Point to a top section and say, "I think that is _____'s head. Turn the middle and bottom sections so that we can find the other pieces to make _____'s whole body."

Expressive Language: Show the child one of the photo strips. Ask the child to identify the classmate in the picture. Encourage the child to talk about what is visible on each strip.

Family Involvement:

Make take-home puzzles of different children in the class as described in "Independent Explorations" above. Put the puzzle pieces into an envelope so that the child can take it home and reconstruct the children's photographs with family members. Encourage the parents to talk with their child about these classmates and what they do together.

SOUND LOTTO

SKILL: SENSORY EXPLORATION—AUDITORY RECEPTION AND MEMORY

OBJECTIVES:

1. To listen carefully to environmental sounds
2. To name the source of each sound
3. To identify the person or object that made the sound
4. To match a photograph of an object with the sound it makes

DESCRIPTION:

Give the class the responsibility for finding 10 to 12 inanimate objects in their environment that make distinctive sounds. Have the group name each object, tell how it is used, and then make the sound. Take a photograph of each object.

Make a game board by using a page layout program to orient the page lengthwise horizontally and to draw one horizontal line and one vertical line to make four boxes. (To make the game more challenging, add two or three vertical lines to make six or eight boxes.) Import one digitized photograph into each box. Print this page. Then create a new game board by deleting one or two pictures and importing others to fill those boxes and then printing it. Laminate each game board.

To play a lotto game, have each child select a game board. Put out buttons or other small objects for use as markers. Ask the children to look at the pictures on their boards. Place the sound-making objects behind a box top or other screen so that they are out of the sight of the children.

Shake or otherwise manipulate one of the objects to create its sound. Ask the children to identify the object that made the sound. If they have a picture of that object on their board, they should cover it with a marker. Continue with other objects. The game is over when a child has covered his or her board completely.

EXTENSIONS:

Small-Group Activities:

Have one child be the sound maker, moving the objects behind the screen while the other children listen for the sounds to complete their game boards.

Independent Explorations:

Make a tape recording of the objects' sounds so that children can play the game independently. To make the recording, arrange the objects near a tape recorder set up with a blank tape. Be sure there is as little background noise as possible. Hold each item

near the microphone and move or otherwise manipulate it for 3 to 5 seconds as it makes its distinctive sound. Let the tape run with 5 to 8 seconds of silence before making the sound of the next object. Repeat until all the objects have been sounded.

Show the children how to play the tape, listen to the object, and then cover its picture on a game board. Then put the setup in the listening center for individual use.

One-on-One Instruction:

Receptive Language: Look at each object with the child. Talk about its distinctive features, what it does, and its name. Then ask the child to listen as you say a word and then to point to the object named.

Expressive Language: Display the objects used in the lotto game. Encourage the child to talk about each one. Ask open-ended questions that will allow the child to express thoughts about the objects at his or her level of development.

Family Involvement:

Send home a cassette tape player, the sound tape, and two game boards. Include directions on how to play the game so that parents can play the game with their child.

Encourage parents to work with their child to collect objects that make distinctive sounds at home. Suggest that they hide the objects from their child's sight, manipulate each object in turn to make its sound, have the child guess what the object is, and then verify each guess by removing the object from hiding and showing it to the child.

GOING ON A TRIP

SKILL: SENSORY EXPLORATION—AUDITORY SEQUENTIAL MEMORY

OBJECTIVES:

1. To listen to a sequence of words
2. To recall a sequence of words

DESCRIPTION:

During a field trip or nature walk, take photographs of objects that are representative of the place being visited. For example, on a trip to a fire station, take a photograph of the building, a fire truck, a hose, a fire hydrant, a firefighter's boots, a firefighter's jacket and helmet, a hatchet, and a fire fighter in uniform.

Once back in class, play a listening game with the children. Teach the children the following rhyme:

> We went to the _____
> And what did we see?
> Here is a list
> As long as can be.
> We saw a . . .

Ask the group to fill in the name of one of the objects they saw on the trip. Then prop up the photo of that object on the chalkboard ledge. Repeat the rhyme with the class, completing the last sentence with that word.

Name a second object and repeat the process, this time listing the two objects in order in the last sentence. Repeat with a third object. Once the group understands how to participate, turn the photo cards away from them until they have listed the objects orally. Then show the sequence to check whether they were correct.

As the children become more proficient, add to the length of the string of words that must be remembered.

EXTENSIONS:

Small-Group Activities:

Make a long inset board so that the photographs can be inserted quickly to create the sequence. Have one child set up the board and hold it so that the others are unable to see the pictures. Tell the leader to say the rhyme. List the words and then challenge the group to recall the sequence. Then have the leader turn the board around to show the correct answer.

Independent Explorations:

Tape-record the rhyme with the string of objects named. Place the tape, a tape player, and other materials for this activity in the work area. The children can take out the photographs, insert and play the cassette tape, and then place the pictures in sequence. Make the tape self-correcting by repeating the rhyme and sequence slowly and asking the child to check.

One-on-One Instruction:

Receptive Language: Lay the photographs on the table and describe one of the objects in the photos. Say, "I'm going to say two words, and I want you hand me the picture for those words in the correct order. Fire truck, boots." The child should hand you the photos of those objects in the correct sequence. Gradually increase the number of words in the sequence.

Expressive Language: Talk with the child about the pictured objects and the experiences of the field trip. Have the child recall the events in order. Then play the memory game described above in "Receptive Language."

Family Involvement:

Write out directions for this simple sequencing game so that parents can play it with their child as the family travels in the car, waits in line, or has a few moments between other activities.

TEXTURE WALK

SKILL: SENSORY EXPLORATION—TACTILE AWARENESS

OBJECTIVES:

1. To identify textures by feel alone
2. To name a variety of different textures
3. To match photographs to their real objects

DESCRIPTION:

Pass around the group a variety of objects that have distinctive textures. Talk about the way these items feel. Tell the group that they are going to go on a texture walk and that their job will be to find as many interesting textures as they can. Mention that each child will get to choose a textured object that you will then photograph.

Back in class, print the pictures and mount them on construction paper. Have the children talk about each texture object; write down what they say. Be sure to elicit from the children a description of the way the object feels. Bind the pages into a *Texture Book* that documents the class texture walk.

EXTENSIONS:

Small-Group Activities:

Work with a small group of children to arrange the object pictures into a slide show that can be viewed on the computer. Once the sequence has been established, the children can record their voices to add a commentary for each photograph.

Independent Explorations:

Print all the object pictures and place them at the work area. The children can take turns grouping the pictures by texture (e.g., rough, smooth, fuzzy).

One-on-One Instruction:

Receptive Language: Place on a table the pictures used in "Independent Explorations" above. Name one texture and direct the child to find a photograph of an object that has that feel. For example, say, "Which one is sharp? . . . Yes, the knife is sharp."

Expressive Language: Look at the *Texture Book* with the child. Ask the child to talk about what is shown on each page. Encourage a description of the texture.

Family Involvement:

Show families the slide show created in "Small-Group Activities." Encourage the families to look for different textures in their own homes and to talk about them with their children.

TOUCH-A-POSTER

SKILL: SENSORY EXPLORATION—TACTILE AWARENESS

OBJECTIVES:

1. To touch a variety of textures
2. To name various textures
3. To identify various textures by touch alone
4. To find objects in the environment that represent named textures

DESCRIPTION:

Explore a variety of textures with the class over the course of several days. Each day, feature a different texture. Bring to circle time some objects of a particular texture. For example, bring a small glass mirror, a drinking glass, and a pair of eyeglasses. Name the objects and pass them around the circle. Once the children have felt the objects, name the texture. Say, "The glass feels *smooth.*"

Have each child locate one object in the immediate environment that represents the texture being studied and take a photograph of it. Print the photographs and have the children paste them onto poster board to form a texture collage for each texture. Label the posters and display them in the room.

EXTENSIONS:

Small-Group Activities:

Import four photographs into a page layout program, each photo representing one of the key textures being explored. Print and laminate these pictures and then cut them into individual cards. Place all the cards face down in a basket. Have one child act as the leader, holding the basket so that another child can draw out a card and name the texture. Then tell the small group to search the room for examples of that texture and to bring them back to the group for inspection.

Independent Explorations:

Print a second set of texture pictures, mount them on cards, and laminate. Label and glue a sample texture swatch onto a shoe box lid for each texture being explored. The children can sort the photo cards by texture into the box lids.

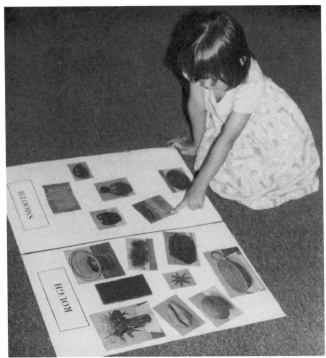

One-on-One Instruction:

Receptive Language: Lay out two objects of different textures. Have the child feel the items. Ask the child to show you the one that represents a specific texture. For example, ask, "Which one is fuzzy?" Once the child can identify all the objects by texture, repeat with the photographs of those objects.

Expressive Language: Show a picture of an object and invite the child to tell you about it. If the child does not include a description of the texture, ask, "What does the feel like?"

Work with the child to make an individual texture book. Glue each picture onto a large index card. Ask the child to tell you about the object in the picture; write down what the child says. Have the child decorate one card as the book cover and bind the cards together into a booklet.

Family Involvement:

Send home a sample of a textured object and one texture object photograph in an envelope with directions. Ask the parents to have their child identify the texture and then look around the house to find objects that match that texture. Invite the child to bring this newfound texture object to school to share with classmates.

Ask the class to find small samples of textures at home to add to the class texture posters.

SNIFF-A-RECIPE

SKILL: SENSORY EXPLORATION—OLFACTORY AWARENESS

OBJECTIVES:

1. To match an odor with its object
2. To identify objects by smell alone

DESCRIPTION:

Choose a recipe, such as gingerbread, that has ingredients with distinctive aromas. Take a photograph of each ingredient; print and mount the photos to make "aroma" cards. Talk with the group about making the recipe and what ingredients will be used. Show the aroma cards and name each item. Use the pictures to make a photo recipe chart.

Place each aromatic ingredient into a small container and cover with a thin piece of towel. Challenge a child to sniff one container gently and to match that smell to its picture. To verify the answer, uncover the real object. Repeat with other children and other food items.

Make the recipe. Ask the group whether any of the individual smells are still present or whether the aroma of the food is entirely new.

EXTENSIONS:

Small-Group Activities:

Put thin pieces of towel and the sample ingredients in their containers at a center. Have one child act as the leader, challenging other children to sniff the containers in turn and to match the smells to their pictures.

Independent Explorations:

Provide three aroma cards and three sets of four containers, each with a small amount of a single food item. Children can sniff the containers and match all the smells to their aroma cards.

One-on-One Instruction:

Receptive Language: Place the aroma cards on the table, facing the child. Let the child smell a lightly covered container with one of the ingredients. Ask the child to iden-

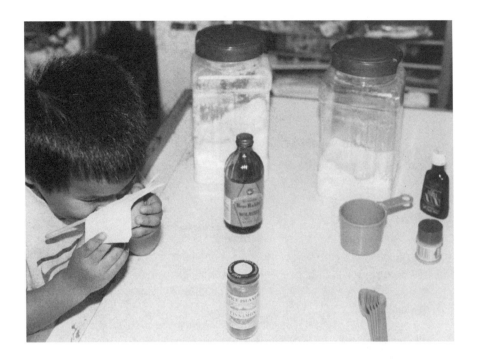

tify the picture of the object that matches that smell. Use the word as you verify the answer. For example, say, "Yes, that's the smell of cinnamon."

Expressive Language: Show the child the aroma cards. Let the child sniff the covered ingredient; then ask the child to name the smell. For example, "That's cinnamon."

Family Involvement:

Encourage parents to include their child in cooking activities at home and to challenge their child to guess what various ingredients are by smell alone.

BY NOSE ALONE

SKILL: SENSORY EXPLORATION—OLFACTORY AWARENESS

OBJECTIVES:

1. To match two containers with the same smell
2. To identify aromas by smell alone

DESCRIPTION:

Place a cotton ball into each of several discarded film containers. Drop a different food extract (e.g., vanilla, cherry, orange, peppermint, almond, mint) or other fragrance (e.g., onion, garlic, peanut butter, perfume, aftershave) onto a separate cotton ball; cover the canisters.

Take a photograph of the real object from which each smell was extracted. Print and mount the object photos on cards.

Display the pictures. Open one of the containers and have a child take a careful whiff and then match the smell to its corresponding picture. For example, the child would match a picture of a candy cane to the peppermint smell.

EXTENSIONS:

Small-Group Activities:

Appoint a leader, who asks for a "sniffer" volunteer and a "blindfold" helper. Tell the helper to tie a blindfold around the sniffer's eyes. Then tell the leader to hold one of the containers under the sniffer's nose and to ask that child to name the aroma.

Independent Explorations:

Place the object cards and aroma containers in the sensory learning center so that children can match smells and pictures.

One-on-One Instruction:

Receptive Language: Place two or three object cards on the table and ask the child to uncap one of the containers. Have the child carefully smell the contents, match it to its picture, and name the smell.

Expressive Language: Lay each object card face down and place its container on top of it. Have the child choose one of the containers, uncap it, and carefully smell the contents. Ask the child to name that smell. The child can self-check the answer by turning over the card.

Family Involvement:

Send home a request for parents to include their young child in meal preparation, talking about the smells of the different ingredients.

MINESTRONE

SKILL: SENSORY EXPLORATION—GUSTATORY AWARENESS

OBJECTIVES:

1. To taste each ingredient used to make a recipe
2. To identify items by taste alone
3. To match a pictured object with its taste

DESCRIPTION:

Prepare to make a recipe, such as minestrone, with the children that features ingredients with distinctive tastes and textures. Have the children in turn taste each item and talk about its flavor and texture. (Use all sanitary precautions—e.g., washing hands and ingredients, using disposable tasting spoons, not sharing tasting spoons—when tasting is done in the classroom. Also check for any food allergies the children may have.)

Take a photograph of each ingredient as it is being prepared for the recipe. Cook or bake the item and take a photograph of the finished product. Have the children share in eating the final product and talking about its taste.

Afterward, print the pictures. Make a game board with two columns. Label one "Soft" and the other "Crunchy." Have the children sort the ingredient photos by texture. Some ingredients will be soft as they are added, such as cooked kidney beans, cooked macaroni, butter, precooked beef, and tomato. Other ingredients will be crunchy as they are added, such as celery, onion, and carrots.

EXTENSIONS:

Small-Group Activities:

Display the game board with ingredients photos. Put out a plate of other foods that are either soft or crunchy, such as peanut butter, pretzels, hard-boiled eggs, and crackers. Tell the children they may eat one of each item and describe its texture. Encourage the children to talk about their taste discoveries at this activity center. (Again, use all necessary sanitation precautions when tasting is done in the classroom.)

Independent Explorations:

Mix up the ingredients cards in a decorative cookie tin. Children can then open it to sort the ingredients cards into categories.

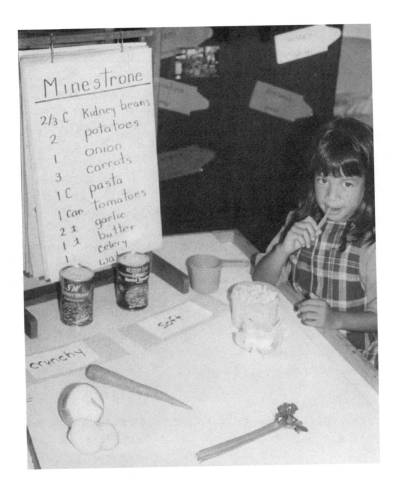

One-on-One Instruction:

Receptive Language: Print a copy of the photograph of each ingredient used in the recipe. Place them in front of the child and ask her to identify all the crunchy ones.

Expressive Language: Once the child has sorted the pictures in the receptive task above, ask her to name each ingredient and to talk about its texture. She could say, "It's a carrot. It was hard and crunchy."

Family Involvement:

Make a picture recipe card for the child to take home. The card would feature the ingredients listed by photograph, name, and quantity. Encourage parents to have their child "read" the recipe at home to different family members and to make the recipe with their child when possible.

SWEET AND SOUR

SKILL: SENSORY EXPLORATION—GUSTATORY AWARENESS

OBJECTIVES:

1. To identify sweet and sour tastes
2. To identify foods that are sweet and foods that are sour
3. To identify facial expressions associated with sweet or sour foods

DESCRIPTION:

Always remember to follow strict food preparation, health, and safety guidelines. Remind children to wash their hands before any cooking or eating activity. Also provide individual disposable tasting utensils.

Select a recipe with distinctly sweet and sour tastes, such as egg rolls with sweet and sour dipping sauce. Have the children taste the key ingredients. Take close-up photographs of individual children tasting an ingredient. On poster board, display a photograph of the object; surround it with the photos of the children tasting it. Make a separate poster for each ingredient.

Repeat with other recipes, such as lemonade, sweet and dill pickles, or pickled beets (using vinegar and sugar).

EXTENSIONS:

Small-Group Activities:

Put one sweet and one sour food in the activity center. Add a mirror and the "tasting" posters described above. Encourage the children to look in the mirror as they taste the food and compare their facial expressions to the ones shown on the posters. (Expect lots of laughter!)

Independent Explorations:

Print a set of "tasting" photographs and mount them on individual cards. Put the cards on a tray with a sweet food, a sour food, and a mirror. Children can taste the food and then find all the photos that show their classmates making a similar face when eating that particular food.

One-on-One Instruction:

Receptive Language: Show two pictures—one showing a child with a pucker while tasting a sour food and another showing a child with a smile while eating something sweet. Ask the child to find the picture of a child eating something sour.

Expressive Language: Give the child a food to sample. Ask the child to name it and then to describe the taste.

Family Involvement:

Let the family know that the class is exploring sweet and sour tastes. Ask the parents to talk about these tastes with their child as they prepare food. Ask that they send in a note naming and describing a sweet or a sour food their child had at home. Add these notes to the class posters.

SENSORY EXPLORATION CHECKLIST

	Baseline	Period 1	Period 2
Child: _____	__/__/__	__/__/__	__/__/__

Visual

To visualize the whole

To identify missing pieces of the whole

To draw the missing piece

To create a whole from various parts

To seek meaningful visual cues

Auditory

To learn to listen intently

To identify objects that make sounds

To identify the direction of a sound

To identify the person or object making a sound

To identify photographs of sources of sounds

To recall the sequence of words or sounds

Tactile

To touch various textures

To identify names of various textures

To identify textures by touch alone

To find objects that represent a named texture

To photograph objects and describe textures

Olfactory

To match an odor with its object

To identify objects by smell alone

To match containers by the smell of their
  contents alone

To identify odors by smell alone

Child: _____

Gustatory

To taste ingredients used in cooking

To identify foods by taste alone

To match a picture of an object to its taste

To identify foods as sweet or sour

To match facial expressions to tastes

CODE:

✔ = Does Consistently

± = Does Sometimes

× = Does Rarely/Does Not Do

8

SCIENCE

SCIENCE INTRODUCTION

What Is Science?

Science is the systematic study of natural phenomena. For young children, science is the exploration and discovery of the physical environment and all the living things that occupy it. Science stimulates curiosity and a sense of wonder in young children, launching them on a quest to understand the world and how it works.

The branches of science explored in this chapter are the physical and life sciences, including physics, chemistry, meteorology, general biology, botany, and zoology.

Why Is Science Education Important?

Science education is important for young children because it encourages them to think. It teaches them to ask questions and then to seek answers to the questions they have formulated.

Science experiences show children how to recognize a problem or phenomenon, form a hypothesis, experiment to test their hypothesis, organize and analyze their data, form tentative conclusions, and then evaluate their results. This process is extremely useful, not only for later science education but also as a framework to examine problems in all areas of life.

How Is Science Learned?

Children are natural explorers. They come into the world full of curiosity and al-most from their first moments are engaged in investigations, making discoveries about their bodies and their environment. Children use their senses to test important scientific concepts like gravity as they drop toast from the high chair, or cause and effect as they tug the string of a pull toy and it moves closer to them.

Science is learning by doing in its purest form. It helps children look closely, listen carefully, identify tastes, discriminate textures by touch alone, and use information gleaned from the sense of smell.

How Is Science Learning Facilitated?

The natural tendency for most adults is to answer with facts a child's questions about the physical world. To encourage scientific thinking, guide children to seek an-swers for themselves and put them in charge of their own investigations.

Fill their environment with materials that invite scientific exploration and stimulate thought. Change these objects frequently to keep the discovery center fresh and chal-lenging. Offer children probing questions about the materials they are examining.

Find out what interests the children about their physical bodies or the world. Listen to their questions on these topics and tie the underlying concepts into the curriculum. Then help children find answers by structuring experiences and providing materials that afford opportunities for investigation and problem solving.

Guide children to use the scientific method. Above all, act as the model of an inquisi-tive adult who is her- or himself actively engaged in investigations and enthusiastic about the process.

WEIGHT FOR ME

SKILL: SCIENCE—PHYSICS

OBJECTIVES:

1. To learn about the force of gravity
2. To experiment with balance and weight
3. To practice meaningful counting skills
4. To improve questioning skills

DESCRIPTION:

Gather the children into a group. Show them a small balance scale and some large and small rocks. Demonstrate how the scale works by putting a large rock on one side and adding several small rocks to the other side until the scale balances. Show them a 2-foot length of 4 × 4-inch lumber and a 6-foot length of 2 × 6-inch lumber. Ask, "Can anyone suggest how to make a balance scale from these two pieces of wood?" Wait for a response and then show how to use the short piece of wood as a fulcrum as you center the long plank on it perpendicularly so that the plank is balanced.

Stand on one end of the plank. That end will touch the ground. Ask the class to guess how many children it will take to balance you on the scale. Invite children to stand on the other end one at a time until the scale balances. Explain that gravity is the invisible force that pulls on objects. Gravity is the reason why objects fall down instead of up. Gravity pulls more strongly on heavier objects. Because an adult is heavier than a child, the teacher stays down until enough children stand on the other side to add weight, thus balancing the scale.

EXTENSIONS:

Small-Group Activities:

In the block building area, provide long wooden planks and cylinders. Encourage children to build a balance scale and to balance it with nothing on either side of the plank. Find several sizes of blocks and let the group experiment with balancing the two sides. The gravitational pull must be the same on both sides in order to balance.

Independent Explorations:

Place pennies, marbles, and other uniformly small objects in separate containers on a table with a balance scale for individual exploration and experimentation.

One-on-One Instruction:

Cut a toilet paper tube in half lengthwise. Put one section, round side up, on a table along with a ruler and a bowl of pennies. Ask the child: "Can you make a balance scale with a ruler?" Invite the child to create a balance scale with the cardboard as the *fulcrum,* or turning point. Instruct the child to balance the ruler on the fulcrum. Challenge the child to balance one penny on each side of the scale. Invite the child to find a small object in the room and to put it on one side of the scale and add enough pennies to the other side to balance the scale. Take a digital photograph of the balancing object and pennies. Print and record the child's exploration of the process involved in achieving the balance.

Family Involvement:

Ask parents to work with their child to make a simple mobile. Suggest that they use a coat hanger, string, and assorted paper shapes with a hole punched in each. *Directions:* Tie one end of differing lengths of string to the bottom wire of the coat hanger. Tie the other end of each string through the hole in a paper shape. Hang the hanger by its hook from a knob or other object. Does the hanger balance? The challenge is to make the bottom of the hanger exactly level by moving the strings with paper shapes attached along the hanger until balance is achieved.

ANIMAL TAILS

SKILL: SCIENCE—ZOOLOGY

OBJECTIVES:

1. To identify animals by their features
2. To match animals with their tails
3. To name body parts of the animals
4. To identify body coverings: fur, feathers, skin, scales

DESCRIPTION:

During an excursion to a farm, pet store, or zoo, take a variety of photographs of the side views of animals. Place each digitized photo into a page layout program, with the body of the animal occupying two-thirds of the page and the tail occupying the other third of the page. Print two copies. Cut one copy of each photograph in two where the tail connects to the body.

Glue the body portion of the animal onto the front part of a paper strip. Pick up the opposite end of the paper strip and fold it in to line up with the back of the body. Crease the paper and glue the tail to the folded portion so that a whole animal is revealed.

Show children the pictures of the animals and ask them to recall the animal names. Discuss physical features and what the children remember about the animals from the excursion.

Show children the picture of an animal without its tail. Ask them to close their eyes and to visualize the tail. Instruct them to open their eyes as you fold the flap forward to reveal the tail for confirmation or correction.

EXTENSIONS:

Small-Group Activities:

Print out an extra copy of animal bodies and tails. Provide the group leader with the photographs of animal bodies. Distribute the animal tail pictures to the other children. Explain that the leader will hold up an animal body picture and that the child with the corresponding tail is to identify the animal and then connect the body picture and tail picture.

Independent Explorations:

Place the fold-out animal body pictures on a table next to a set of animal tail pictures. Children can practice finding the tail that matches the animal body and check for accuracy by folding out the tail section of the strip.

One-on-One Instruction:

Show the child only the tail picture of an animal. Have the child guess what animal it belongs to before showing the body picture. Talk about body coverings: fur (mammals), feathers (birds), skin (e.g., mammals, amphibians), scales (e.g., fish, reptiles).

Family Involvement:

Send home a note asking parents to find pictures of animals in magazines. Suggest that they name the animal and discuss the physical features with their child and then use an index card to cover up a portion of an animal's body and have the child identify what animal it is.

MAGNETIC CHALLENGE

SKILL: SCIENCE—MAGNETISM

OBJECTIVES:

1. To experiment with magnets, discovering items that magnets attract and do not attract
2. To use prediction skills
3. To participate in cooperative learning

DESCRIPTION:

Magnets attract certain metals and objects that contain those metals. After children have freely explored magnets by testing objects that the magnets attract and do not attract, help them generalize their findings.

Invite children to search the classroom for small objects they wish to test with magnets. Gather approximately 15 objects. Take individual photographs of the objects. Print out the pictures and mount them on index cards. Laminate the picture cards and stack them together.

Bring a magnet, the objects, and the pictures to group time. Show the children an object picture card. Ask them to guess whether the magnet will attract the object pictured. After they guess yes or no, test the real object with the magnet.

EXTENSIONS:

Small-Group Activities:

Gather a group of three or four children. Place the real objects and a magnet in the middle of the group along with the stack of picture cards. Invite a child to draw the top card, look at the picture, and guess, by saying yes or no, whether the magnet will attract the object. If no one challenges her, she keeps the card, and the next child takes a turn. If someone challenges the guess, the challenger uses the magnet to test the real object. If correct, he keeps the card; if not, the player keeps the card. Continue playing until all cards in the stack have been used.

Independent Explorations:

Place a magnet and objects on a table for exploration.

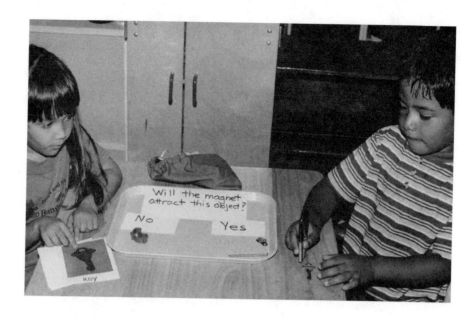

One-on-One Instruction:

Supply the child with a group of objects, the object pictures, and a magnet. Make a large two-column graph with the words "Yes" and "No" at the top. Invite the child to guess whether the magnet will attract the object pictured and then to test the real object by using the magnet. Place the picture of the object on the graph in the correct column.

Family Involvement:

Send home a magnet with instructions. Ask the family to encourage the child to test objects around the home to discover what the magnet will attract. Ask that parents write down what objects their child tested and the results and to return this information to school for sharing.

HEALTHFUL SNACK PARTNERS

SKILL: SCIENCE—BIOLOGY

OBJECTIVES:

1. To learn how good nutrition promotes health
2. To identify fruits and vegetables
3. To eat fruits and vegetables
4. To participate in cooperative learning activities

DESCRIPTION:

After exploring a unit of study on food and nutrition, discuss with the group the importance of eating at least five servings of fruits and vegetables a day. Ask the children to name their favorite fruits and vegetables.

Wash and then cut two fruits and two vegetables into bite-sized pieces. Take a photograph of an individual piece of each fruit and vegetable. Import each digitized photograph into a page layout program that duplicates the picture four times on a page. Print them out and cut them into four cards. Mount each picture on card stock and laminate. You should end up with 16 picture cards—4 for each fruit and vegetable.

Place the cut-up fruits and vegetables on a platter on the snack table. Stand wooden skewers in a cup. Place the picture cards in a basket on the table.

Invite a child to pick a snack partner; tell both partners to wash their hands. Explain that one child will choose four to six picture cards and place them in order, left to right, on the snack table and that the partner will match the pictures with the real fruits and/or vegetables, threading them in order on a wooden skewer. Let the children reverse roles and then eat the snack.

EXTENSIONS:

Small-Group Activities:

Make a duplicate set of the 16 fruit and vegetable cards. Invite two children to play a card game. Deal four cards to each child and place the rest of the stack in the middle of the table. Explain that the objective is to get as many sets of matching cards as possible. Play like the game of Go Fish, but require only two matching cards to make a set.

Independent Explorations:

Place the fruit and vegetable cards on a table for sorting and patterning.

One-on-One Instruction:

Begin a pattern with the fruit and vegetable picture cards. Start with a simple A-B pattern and ask the child to extend it. Proceed with more challenging patterns according to ability and interest.

Family Involvement:

Send home a copy of the fruit and vegetable cards with instructions for creating and extending patterns. Suggest that parents and their child take turns creating and extending the pattern.

WHAT GROWS?

SKILL: SCIENCE—BOTANY

OBJECTIVES:

1. To develop a beginning understanding of living and nonliving things
2. To discover that plants grow
3. To discover that plants need water and light to grow
4. To develop scientific thinking, using observation, prediction, and testing skills
5. To name basic parts of a plant

DESCRIPTION:

Collect a kidney bean, penny, marble, sunflower seed, rock, and popcorn kernel.

Take a photograph of each item. Insert a photo into a page layout program, centering the photo at the top of the page. Add two columns under the photograph, one labeled "No" and the other labeled "Yes." Repeat with the other photos and print out a hard copy of each chart.

Bring the above six items, photograph charts, six small plastic lunch bags, potting soil, and a pitcher of water to the group area. Tell the children that you want them to predict what will grow. Identify each item, place it into a bag of potting soil, and ask, "Will this _____ grow?" If a child thinks it will grow, she should sign her name in the "Yes" column under the picture; if not, she should sign under the "No" column.

After all the children have made their hypotheses, pour a small amount of water into each plastic bag and hang them from a clothesline attached to a window frame. Attach the photograph with the predictions next to the appropriate bag.

Check the bags daily for growth, ending the experiment after 2 weeks. Check children's predictions and actual outcomes. As the seeds sprout and grow, point out the various plant parts: roots (the first parts to emerge from the seed), stem, and leaves. Help children form conclusions about what kinds of things grow. Discuss the difference between living and nonliving things.

EXTENSIONS:

Small-Group Activities:

Invite each small group of children to work together in planting two lima beans. Each group should plant one of two beans in a clear plastic cup with soil and add water. One cup should be placed in a sunny place and the other in a dark place. Teams can check their beans daily for growth. Remind the children to water the beans regularly to keep them moist.

Take photographs of the planted beans every day for 2 weeks. Print out the photos and write the number of the day in the upper right-hand corner of the page. Ask the children to describe what they see, naming the parts of the plant. Record their responses below the pictures each day. At the end of 2 weeks, gather the two sets of pictures and have the children draw conclusions about sunlight and plant growth.

Independent Explorations:

Invite children to help care for the school garden by planting, watering, weeding, and harvesting as needed.

One-on-One Instruction:

Invite the child to find something on the playground or to bring an item from home that he thinks will grow. Provide soil, a cup, a small pitcher of water, and a marker. Ask the child to write his name and the name of the item on the cup before planting. Give the child the responsibility of caring for the plant and of watching for growth. Record results after 2 weeks. Ask the child to evaluate whether or not his initial hypothesis was correct.

Family Involvement:

Send home a note asking parents to look around their home, yard, or neighborhood with their child to find something the child thinks might grow. Ask that they send the item to school for planting and watching for growth.

HOW'S THE WEATHER?

SKILL: SCIENCE—METEOROLOGY

OBJECTIVES:

1. To become aware of the weather by looking at the sky
2. To identify the characteristics of weather conditions
3. To describe and graph weather data

DESCRIPTION:

Check the weather each morning with the children. Each day, take a photograph of the same area, which should include the sky and a tree, other plant, or wind sock.

Have the children describe the weather by looking at the picture. Ask:

What does the sky look like?
How does it feel outside?
What kind of clothes do you wear in this weather?
What can you do and what can't you do in this type of weather?

EXTENSIONS:

Small-Group Activities:

Make a computerized page that creates multiple copies of the same picture for each of the five types of weather in your region. Cut them up to use on a calendar. After the children determine the weather for each day, attach the matching small photograph to the corresponding spot on the calendar. At the end of each week, have the children count and determine the most prevalent type of weather.

Independent Explorations:

Provide page-sized graphs with pictures of the five different types of weather (sunny, cloudy, windy, rainy, snowy) indicated on the vertical axis, and the number of days indicated on the horizontal axis. The children can graph the weather over a week or month by counting and recording the number of sunny, cloudy, windy, rainy, or snowy days.

One-on-One Instruction:

Play a guessing game with the child. Ask the child to guess what type of weather you are thinking of. Give clues about sky conditions, temperature, appropriate dress, and activities for the weather in question.

Family Involvement:

Send home a set of five weather pages, each with a picture of a different type of weather. Instruct the parents to talk with their child about the weather pictured and to ask questions such as, "What do you like about this kind of weather?" and "What can you do on this kind of day?" Suggest that family members record the child's responses and bind the pages together to make a weather book.

THE STEPS OF PLANTING

SKILL: SCIENCE—BOTANY

OBJECTIVES:

1. To discover that plants are alive and grow
2. To discover that most plants have roots, stems, and leaves
3. To follow a sequence of directions
4. To develop observation skills

DESCRIPTION:

Take photographs of the following five steps of obtaining and planting a plant slip. Make one set of these photos for each child as instructions:

1. Using a pencil to poke a hole in the potting soil
2. Using scissors to cut a stem off a potted plant
3. Dipping the cut end of the cut stem (slip) into a bowl of water
4. Dipping the cut end of the slip into rooting compound
5. Placing the slip into the previously made hole in the soil

Place the photographic instructions next to the materials needed, in order, around a table. Invite the children to follow the sequence of instructions to obtain and plant a slip.

Take a digital photograph of the child at each station. Put it into a page layout that divides the page into five equal strips horizontally. Print two copies for each child for use in activities described below.

EXTENSIONS:

Small-Group Activities:

Two or three children work together at a table, each cutting apart their own five strips depicting the planting sequence. Ask them to collaborate to create a picture story of the planting process by recalling the steps involved. Suggest that they use at least one strip from each person in the group, line them up in order from left to right, and then glue the chosen strips to a 4-foot length of 12-inch-wide butcher paper. Encourage the children to discuss the process, describing what is happening in the photographs. Record their responses below the pictures.

Independent Explorations:

Put potting soil in a large plastic tub on a table in the sensory center. Place a variety of beans, some plant cuttings, and small garden tools next to the tub. Allow children to experiment with digging and planting.

One-on-One Instruction:

Instruct the child to cut apart her five photographs. Mix up the photographs and have her put them in order, recalling the steps of planting. Afterward, direct the child to put the photographs in an envelope and label it with her name.

Family Involvement:

Send home the five photo strips previously cut by the child at school. Include a note to the parents: Ask your child to recall the sequence of the process. Have him paste the photographs in order on a paper strip. Ask him to describe what he is doing in each picture and write his words below the pictures. Send this project back to school for sharing with the class.

RISING TO THE OCCASION

SKILL: SCIENCE—CHEMISTRY

OBJECTIVES:

1. To gain a beginning understanding of gases and the expansion of gases
2. To observe changes that occur in the expansion of gases
3. To gain an understanding of the three states of matter: solid, liquid, gas

DESCRIPTION:

Conduct this introductory demonstration of inflating a balloon with baking soda and vinegar. First, let the children touch the baking soda; say, "This is baking soda. It is solid matter." Let the children dip their fingers in vinegar (Make sure fingers have no cuts; vinegar will make cuts sting!); say, "This is vinegar. It is liquid matter." Next, use a funnel to pour baking soda into a bottle that has a small opening. Then pour in some vinegar and quickly stretch the mouth of a balloon over the opening. The balloon will inflate. Ask the children what made the balloon inflate—a solid, a liquid, or a gas. Point out the bubbles in the bottle and discuss the chemical reaction that occurred when vinegar was added to the soda. The gas called carbon dioxide was given off and inflated the balloon.

Photograph each step in making a recipe for bread. Take photographs of mixing all the ingredients, including yeast, together, letting the dough rise, punching the dough down, and letting it rise again before putting the bread into the oven to bake.

Print the photographs of the bread-making process and mount them on a poster board, creating a photographic recipe. Number the steps and laminate the board. Post it in the cooking area and invite children to help make bread by following the recipe. As children notice the bread rising, make sure they look closely at the bubbles in the dough; discuss gas formation. When punching down the dough, point out the escape of gas. After cooking the bread, slice it and point out the holes, caused by the gas, in the bread. Then let the children eat the bread.

Recall with the group the steps and the process by looking at the photographs. Discuss how the bread rose and the role of yeast in making gas.

EXTENSIONS:

Small-Group Activities:

Read to the group the story "The Little Red Hen" and invite children to act out the steps the hen took to get ready to make bread. Show the children the recipe pictures; ask them to identify the solids and liquids and to recall what they did. Record their responses.

Independent Explorations:

Put baby food jars, spoons, baking soda, and vinegar on a discovery table. Encourage children to explore the substances and to experiment with mixing the baking soda and vinegar.

One-on-One Instruction:

Resize the photographs of the bread recipe to 2 × 3 inches each and print them out. Instruct the child to arrange the pictures in correct order for making the recipe. Allow the child to glue the photos onto a sheet of paper to take home.

Family Involvement:

Send home the child's picture recipe with a note to the parents directing them to ask their child about each step and to write her or his words under each picture, paying special attention to the pictures of the rising dough.

MAGIC CRYSTALS

SKILL: SCIENCE—CHEMISTRY

OBJECTIVES:

1. To notice the changes in states of matter
2. To practice prediction skills
3. To notice changes
4. To increase observation skills

DESCRIPTION:

Fill a clean glass bottle with very hot tap water. Add several teaspoonfuls of sugar to the hot water and stir. Continue adding sugar and stirring until no more sugar will dissolve. Cut a length of string that is a few inches longer than the height of the bottle. Tie one end of the string to a paper clip. Tie the other end of the string around the middle of a pencil. Place the pencil across the top of the bottle, with the paper clip hanging into the bottle. Wind the string around the pencil until the paper clip hangs just above the bottom of the bottle.

Take a digital photograph of the bottle with the sugar solution and string. Print it and place it at the top of a prediction chart labeled from Day 1 through Day 5. Ask the children to guess how many days they think it will take for crystals to form; then have them sign their names under the number of days they predict.

Take a digital photograph of the bottle of sugar solution every day at the same time. Print and display the photo above the numbered day. Remind the children to look for changes and crystal formation. Guide the children to compare their predictions with the results observed and recorded in the photograph.

EXTENSIONS:

Small-Group Activities:

Leave the bottle of growing crystals on the table for several days after the experiment. Suggest that the children continue to observe. Record the crystal growth with digital photographs. Then take the string out of the water and place the crystals on a small dish. Invite children to examine the crystals with a magnifying lens, or place a few crystals on a microscope slide and let the children view them with a microscope.

Independent Explorations:

Place sugar, salt, and sand in open containers on a table in the discovery area. Provide a magnifying lens, microscope slides, and a microscope. Invite children to examine the crystals, noting that each different substance has its own crystal shape.

One-on-One Instruction:

Place the containers of sugar, salt, and sand on a table and take a digital photograph of each one. Import each photo into a page layout program, placing the photo at the top of the page. Print and label the three photographs. Ask the child to examine and describe each crystal. Record the responses on the page below the corresponding photograph.

Family Involvement:

Put in an envelope for parents a 12-inch length of string, a paper clip, and directions for growing crystals as done in the "Description" above. Suggest that they add food coloring to the water as they try the activity with their child or try to grow a different type of crystal by stirring salt or washing soda into the hot water instead of sugar. Ask the parents to help their child record the growth of the crystals. Invite the child to bring the cluster of crystals to school to share with classmates.

SCIENCE TALK

SKILL: SCIENCE—SCIENTIFIC TERMS

OBJECTIVES:

1. To understand the meanings of scientific words
2. To act out the meanings of scientific terms
3. To use new scientific vocabulary appropriately in conversation

DESCRIPTION:

Make scientific vocabulary meaningful to young children by first explaining it and then having them act it out. For example, when studying butterflies, expose the group to the *proboscis* through which the butterfly drinks plant nectar. Costumes for butterflies could include headbands with pipe cleaner antennae. Give each child butterfly a party favor that unrolls when it is blown. Show the children how to fly close to the blossom of a plastic plant and then extend the proboscis to pretend to drink a drop of liquid from the flower.

Take photographs of the dramatization so that children are able to print out copies to put into their individual word banks.

EXTENSIONS:

Small-Group Activities:

Work with a few children at a time to make individual science word banks. For each child, print out a set of key science pictures from the lesson being studied (e.g., a caterpillar, a chrysalis, antennae, a proboscis). Have the children name and talk about each of the pictures as they cut them out and paste them onto 5 × 7-inch index cards. Print the words for the children, naming the letters as they watch the letters being formed. Bind each set of cards together by punching holes in them and securing with a book ring.

Independent Explorations:

Put costumes for the new vocabulary words into the dramatic play center with a mirror and the photo cards made in the "Small-Group Activities" above.

One-on-One Instruction:

Share the props for the new vocabulary words with the child and then look at the photographs. Name one of the new words and ask the child to find it in the picture. For example, say, "Find the proboscis on the butterfly."

Review the photo vocabulary cards in the child's word bank, asking the child to name the objects pictured.

Family Involvement:

Send home a duplicate set of some of the child's new words from the word bank. Ask the parents to sit with their child and listen to the description of the words and what was done at school to learn about them.

SCIENCE CHECKLIST

	Baseline	Period 1	Period 2

Child: _____ __/__/__ __/__/__ __/__/__

Scientific Method

To observe
To question
To develop predictive skills
To test a hypothesis
To work cooperatively in discovery
To use scientific terms

Zoology

To name animals
To identify animal body parts
To identify body coverings: fur, feathers, skin, scales
To identify animals by their features

Physics

To learn about the force of gravity
To explore balance
To experiment with a lever

Physical Science

To experiment with magnets
To identify materials that magnets attract

Biology

To learn about nutrition
To learn how good nutrition promotes health

	Baseline	Period 1	Period 2
Child: _____	_/_/_	_/_/_	_/_/_

Botany

To distinguish between living and nonliving things

To understand the process and steps of plant growth

To learn that plants need light and water

To name basic plant parts

Meteorology

To become aware of various weather conditions

To name various weather conditions

To describe different weather conditions

To graph weather conditions

Chemistry

To categorize states of matter as solid, liquid, or gas

To experiment with gases

To observe transformation from solid to liquid or gas

To notice the changes in states of matter

CODE:

✔ = Does Consistently

± = Does Sometimes

× = Does Rarely/Does Not Do

INDEX

CORWIN
PRESS

The Corwin Press logo—a raven striding across an open book—represents the happy union of courage and learning. We are a professional-level publisher of books and journals for K–12 educators, and we are committed to creating and providing resources that embody these qualities. Corwin's motto is "Success for All Learners."